Eugene Poston

Shelby, N. C.

E. Eugene Poston, President
Gardner-Webb College
Boiling Springs, N. C.

D1418119

THE FLAME OF LIFE

THE
FLAME
OF
LIFE

An Interpretation of

the Sermon on the Mount

by

ERIC MONTIZAMBERT

GREENWICH
CONNECTICUT
1955

COPYRIGHT 1955 BY THE SEABURY PRESS,
INCORPORATED
LIBRARY OF CONGRESS CATALOG CARD
NUMBER: 55-8740
PRINTED IN THE UNITED STATES OF AMERICA

Gift of E. Eugene Poston, President
Gardner-Webb College
Boiling Springs, N. C.

BT
380
M58

2-16-77

To

JESSE IRVING SLOAT, M.D., F.A.C.S.,
> devoted Christian, great surgeon, beloved friend,

> and in precious memory of

IDA BELLE, his wife,
> whose faith and love live ever with us.

PREFACE

Although this essay should prove to be easy reading, I trust that no one who takes it up will ever again think of the message of Jesus as "a simple Gospel" or fall into the deadly trap set by some sentimentalists who forget that there is no true Christianity apart from the Church, the Body of Christ. Consequently, the entire fabric of the thinking exposed in these pages is integrated with the historic New Testament ideal of the Christian Church as "the New Israel of God"—the Christian synagog, the reformed yet continuing faith of the Old Testament. The Sermon on the Mount reveals an ethic, the rule of life designed by our Lord for the members of His Body, and to be attained only by the grace of God. But it is only in the broader picture of the "New Israel," rising out of the essential unity of Old and New Testament faith and doctrine, that alone may be found the key to redemption. To think of Jesus Christ as a simple moralist, albeit the master of them all, is to betray mankind to that secularism which already exhibits its futility in the current collapse of civilization. The popular fantasy of the rugged Man of Nazareth offering a code of morals as the antidote for spiritual death must be abandoned. Conversion is the one panacea for decay. Faith in the Eternal God Incarnate—living, dying, rising from the dead—is man's first and last hope of salvation from himself.

The whole of this small book has been written on "days off" at my rural retreat and without reference to any of the standard commentaries. It was so done for the sake of freshness, and with no desire to contribute to the edification of scholars in the New Testament field. In truth, I have written for the people of God who in these bitter days yearn for a deeper understanding of the basic things in the faith of man's redemption. Always I have tried to say, "Not I, but the Lord!" It should be obvious enough that I have spoken in these pages as I speak to my Friday "lay folks Bible Class." I have learned much from their comments, criticisms, and practical insights. Where there are references to the fruits of contemporary scholarship—the inescapable *bête noir* of the writer on religion—these are dictated by necessity.

Except in a few cases where the easily recognizable King James Version has been quoted, the biblical text used has been taken from the Revised Standard Version of the Bible, copyrighted 1946 and 1952 and used by permission. As usual, I am greatly indebted to my wife, Winifred, for her lucid counsels, especially in the section devoted to prayer and the Our Father. Here her mind alone has been my commentary on the sacred text.

—Eric Montizambert

CONTENTS

PREFACE   vii

CHAPTER   I   Primary Facts and Principles   I

CHAPTER   II   The Beatitudes and the Woes   22
               Matthew 5:1-12 and Luke 6:17-26

CHAPTER   III The Law and the Gospel   49
               Matthew 5:17-20 and Luke 16:17

CHAPTER   IV   Specific Laws in the New
               Light   56
               Matthew 5:21-48

CHAPTER   V   The Flame of Life   79
               Matthew 6

CHAPTER   VI   New Answers to Old Ques-
               tions   101
               Matthew 7

THE FLAME OF LIFE

CHAPTER I

PRIMARY FACTS AND PRINCIPLES

The Gospel of Christ is a program for crisis. It was given to man at one of the most crucial hours of history when new worlds were in the making. But, unlike many popular causes which have ridden the tide of change, this crusade was itself the dominant factor in the revolution that struck down the Roman eagles in favor of the Cross. It is true, of course, that the Latin empire's sun already was setting when Jesus, an unknown carpenter from the corrupting crossroad's town of Nazareth, began His mission. The historian, thinking backward as he must, may speculate as to the probable fate of Rome had Christianity not intervened. Probably the empire would have collapsed under the battling of rival claimants to its throne. Probably the segmented remnants, heart-rotted by social vice and political opportunism, would have met swift death at the hands of barbarians rushing in to exact vengeance for their own humiliations—no totalitarian power, its unity once broken, can hope long to survive.

But all this is guess work. Jesus burst into the frame of history-in-the-making so silently that He was almost unnoticed. Only a handful of Palestinian peasants and poor townsmen really listened to Him. None but some unscrupulous hierarchs of the family religion cared enough to persecute Him. Though He was the scion of a royalty politically forgotten, He was "a nobody," lost in the midst of a beaten and hopeless nation. Jews were tolerated for a while longer by the Empire, even though governors and procurators were often irritated by irresponsible patriots who called themselves "Messiahs." Socially secure leaders, however, preferred peace to freedom and were ready to play quiet politics with their benign oppressors. At any rate, revolt was hopeless. It was better to be a safe, overtaxed subject than a dead Jew, especially when death came to such rebels through crucifixion.

Into such an unpromising situation, Jesus came with a message apparently quiet and simple, yet potentially aflame with the spirit of moral and spiritual revolution. None could listen to Him with understanding and fail to sense the inevitable consequences of His mission should success come to it. Had Rome known Him, it would have feared greatly, and have destroyed Him of its own accord; for His message, startling in its power, originality, and insight, was destined to undermine the whole moral and spiritual fabric of that state.

Yet Jesus had no political philosophy as such. The

message which the poor and the oppressed, the intellectually alert and the spiriutally eager soon began to call the Good News held no brief for any of the political ideologies of that day or this. Although it is clear enough that certain social, political, and economic systems cannot exist among a Christian people, it is equally certain that the Gospel of Christ—the Revelation housed in the New Testament—does not directly sponsor any ancient or any current form of human government. The mass of slow-thinking followers who abandoned Him when the riotous procession of Palm Sunday was followed by the horror of Calvary did so because He refused to be "a patriot" of the violent nationalist sort. And later, Rome persecuted the disciples because they dared to make His saying, "My Kingdom is not of this world," their own.

Jesus was the one true humanitarian of all time. Nations as such, however great, did not concern Him. His love and care was for men as men, whoever or wherever they were. When one studies the words of Jesus, nothing becomes so quickly evident as the fact that "the Good News of Jesus Christ the Son of God" is the universal Gospel. The reality of the Fatherhood of God—a principle fully realized by Israel's greatest prophets—resolves itself into the practical ideal of the brotherhood of man. And this brotherhood, Jesus teaches, can be realized only if and when the Kingdom of God becomes the complete and the final object of each man's allegiance.

Certainly, the reign of God-in-Christ will come to pass. Careful students of the New Testament are coming more and more to the realization that if man, failing to accept the Gospel, finally rejects the faith of the Redeemer, the Kingdom will come in some climactic intervention of the power and righteousness of God. Perhaps the present horrific clashing of the nations in an increasing godlessness is evidence of this. We may be at the threshold of the end. Who knows? But Jesus warned the disciples against all such speculation. They were to occupy themselves utterly with the proclamation of His message of redemption. By practice, they were to learn to live its life that they might teach it to all men everywhere. By belief in Him, they were to find all that God is to men, as well as knowledge that the living of a redeemed life was possible. To this end, He gave them the secret of faith and, with it, the mode of behavior that became known as Christian conduct.

The principles of Christian behavior are to be found scattered throughout the New Testament, particularly within the four Gospels. Many of their key points, though by no means all, are compacted within the short framework of the Sermon on the Mount. But here take warning! This so-called sermon is not Christianity. With all its power, wonder, and glory, it is but an essential codification of some vital primary precepts concerning the living of the believing life.

Thus it is not the forerunner, but the aftermath, of faith in Christ.

But Is There a Sermon on the Mount?

Is the Sermon on the Mount a sermon? This, of course, is the first question to be answered. Not only is the technical student of the New Testament text required to deal with it, but the ordinary believer must also realize the significance of the question if he is to understand and uphold the faith of his fathers. After all, has he not been taught that the Sermon, the vital words of Jesus, contains "the very heart and soul of Christianity itself"? Indeed, many of his teachers may actually have told him that to "win eternal life" he need do no more than live up to the sublime ethical precepts so briefly stated in the fifth, sixth, and seventh chapters of The Gospel According to St. Matthew. "This do, and thou shalt live!"

The matter, however, is not quite so simple. Even a swift reading of these chapters brings the realization that they set a level of faith and behavior so exalted that no ordinary man can hope to scale its heights. Here is sublimity indeed! Here is a standard of living to which none may lift himself by his own bootstraps. Here, surely, is sainthood in action! That is as true as it is obvious. Yet the very truth of it opens the windows of the mind to the vast sweeping vistas of Jesus' teaching above, other than, and beyond the special principles compressed into what pious tradition (never the Bible) calls the Sermon on the Mount. There is so much else to the redeeming Gospel of Christ, so much that is really more primary and more simple, so much which holds the keys to the grasping of these ideals of holiness that they lose their first appearance of inaccessibility to street-level people.

Jesus never put Himself above the reach of the very common man. Paradox though it seems, the great sayings which challenged the learning of the lawyers and sounded the depths of the philosophers were meat and drink to peasants and fishermen. And the pure humaneness of His heart brought Him closer to the prostitute than to the rabbi. All this, and the "why" of it, will find its explanation at a later stage in our discussion. At the moment, we are concerned with the question which heads this section—Is there a Sermon on the Mount? But even as we ask it, we are halted by yet another which demands immediate reply: What are the four magnificent little books which the infant Church, with its inspired instinct for the right word, named "the Gospels"?

Not so long ago, it was generally assumed that the Gospels were four separate and independent biographies of Jesus of Nazareth. To be sure, readers always were disappointed by the scant supply of traditional biographical material within the records, and scholars were bothered by the different writers' apparent scorn of chronological order. Yet, on these as

sources, professional biographers determined to produce "lives" of Jesus, issued innumerable volumes in
which brilliant scenic descriptions and highly imagina-
tive speculations told us little that we wanted to know
—unless we could be content with luminous background material. Even Dean Farrar's still popular *Life
of Christ,* despite its literary beauty and its thrilling
dramatics, now seems to be a colorful and turgid stage
setting for widely separated appearances of the Star of
stars who does bit pieces of incredible intensity: the
acts and words which were, indeed, the Good News
itself!

But the study, not the content, of the writings has
changed. Now we have recovered something of the
understanding with which the ancient fathers received the books. The fact that they were so much
closer to the events seems to have given them a more
profound and realistic knowledge of the vivid little
evangelistic pamphlets attributed to Matthew, Mark,
Luke, and John. They knew that these were emergency documents, written under high pressure for the
purpose of conserving and presenting the key notes—
only the key notes!—of the apostolic preaching about
Jesus, the Messiah, as Redeemer-God and King of
man and his universe.

The evangelists who wrote the first three of these
"campaign" pamphlets could not have written full
biographies even if they would. They were aflame
with the soul-shaking preaching about the Christian

imperative which literally drove the first disciples to
the ends of their earth. Here alone, among all the
religions and philosophies of men, present and future,
was the solitary hope of the fallen race. Here, without
possibility of doubt, was the Creator-Lord's final proclamation of the swift coming of His Kingdom that
was to replace "with power and great glory" in a
sweeping, mighty judgment all the states and powers
of man's making. Though "wars and rumors of wars"
might soon break into a universal holocaust because
defiant man would scorn His message, it was for them,
the first converts, to bring the good news of redemption through faith in the loving Saviour to all who
would hear. Thus, with the tremendous load of personal evangelism heavy upon them, the apostolic
preachers and teachers had no time for writing. They
thought that the end of all earthly things might come
in their lifetime. And, so too, the authors, who thirty
years later and more, put into script on strips of frail
papyrus the story as they learned it from the preaching.

That, precisely, is what these tracts do. It is why
St. Mark begins his striking, compact treatment of the
doings and speakings of Jesus with the words: "The
beginning of the gospel of Jesus Christ, the Son of
God." He had long listened to the rough, strong
preaching of the heroic Peter. His own mother's house
had been the secret meeting place of the disciples,
once the Resurrection had dissolved their doubts. He

intimately knew the whole story and, knowing it so well, succumbed with the rest of them to the imperative of swift and daring action. So, too, St. Matthew and St. Luke; the latter a later convert of St. Paul in distant Macedonia. Howsoever they heard the Good News, these writing evangelists, with Mark's booklet and a handful of other records, sought only to produce effectual instruments for "the preaching," as they called it. Thus these little books—you can read Mark within the hour—were themselves summaries of selected preaching and teachings of the first disciples, striving within their imperiled lifetimes to win the world to its Creator, Redeemer, and King. Only St. John, writing long afterward, sensed the fact that the end was not yet. But he, too, realized that the ultimate establishment of the Kingdom of God was within the divine plan of salvation.

It should now be clear that the Gospels, taken together, are far from being a complete presentation of the acts and words of Jesus. Indeed, the author of the Fourth Gospel takes pains to assure us that were all that He did and taught to be written down, "the world itself could not contain the books that would be written" (John 21:25). That, to be sure, is the utterance of poetic license; but its truth is amply demonstrated in the fact that scholars skilled in textual and historical criticism are unable to account for more than sixty actual days out of the total ministry of our Lord. What an overwhelming intensity of thought and of action this suggests! Who can imagine any man of ordinary strength and brilliance accomplishing so much in so brief a space? If only we had the full account of the thousand and more days of the full life! But what we do have, in its turn, almost over-matches our capacities for faith and action.

Certainly, the preaching, teaching, and writing dis-ciples were conscious of the tremendous nature of their task. Yet they had to do it, or be false to their trust. What, then, could they do but select from the vast storehouse of materials those words and those deeds most pertinent to their purpose and our need? Inevitably, they had to summarize much that they had come to know by heart, much that already had been incorporated in the rhythmical liturgical worship of the nascent Church. Those were days in which, as in the Middle Ages, people habitually committed to memory as much as a modern actor must master in the full course of his career. And, of course, much that He uttered had to be reduced to easily remem-bered paragraphs and sentences. This, then, is what the great Sermon on the Mount really is: not a ser-mon at all, but a skilled compaction of something in-finitely greater in size, if not in ideas.

The early Christians were under a compulsion more pressing than the simple loyalty of men to the teach-ing of One to whom personal devotion had grown into adoration. Here there was something which transcended at once their individual convictions, as well as Jesus' own conception of His Deity. No thoughtful reading of the Gospels permits us to escape the knowledge that He was overshadowed by a sense of mission to the Old Israel: not merely to reform it, not to replace it, but through an infusion of the divine grace to transform it into the New Israel of God. He was to redeem men through the redemption of the ancient faith, whose leaders had so nearly lost the vision of the mission to which they were called. That heroic faith—corrected, refreshed, enlarged into the recovery of its lost true messianic consciousness—was to be the instrument for the salvation of mankind. It might seem, in the sight of men, to die; but that dying was to be a metamorphosis, a "new birth unto righteousness."

So these men—first the intensively trained Twelve and then their converts—were never unaware of their dedication to the task of spreading the good news of the re-creation of the New Israel, the Church, the Body of Christ of which He, the Eternal Son of Man, had ever been the Head. They garnered the ripened grain which He had sown in word and deed, and gave its essence to all who had ears to hear. Hence, the meticulous care with which they worked. Hence, the accuracy with which they preserved the very heart of His teaching. Hence, the flaming passion with which they projected the message in their own teaching and preaching. And that, indeed, is the function of the living Church, without which there is no salvation.

The Nature of the Sermon

Nothing that we have said is intended to imply that Jesus never spoke all of the words given as the Sermon in The Gospel According to St. Matthew, or that He did not utter them all on one occasion. But it is certain that this particular Gospel offers us something less than the full story. This becomes clear the instant we examine St. Luke's report of the same teaching. Though, on the whole, the contents and significance of the passages occurring in both Gospels are essentially the same, there are verbal variations not to be attributed to an inevitable failure in the listener's memory. Moreover, not only is the Lukan order of the sayings often quite different, but it also gives us striking sentences, ignored, forgotten, squeezed out for lack of space, or altered in the Matthean version. Chiefly, these are differences of addition and omission rather than of contradiction, even though a degree of individual and inescapable interpretation is occasionally obvious. Sometimes these writers, either trusting to their own fallible memories or listening to the slightly varying reports of eyewitnesses, probably were compelled to clarify what seemed to be obscure. Possibly they even hazarded a guess about a missing word. Certainly, they must have puzzled over the differences in the order of the "sayings" that different men reported. Yet these things, after all, were minor, and for us they but serve to reveal the immensity and the grandeur of the messages spoken on the mountain and the plain. However inadequate these reports, based on human memorizings, may seem to be, they caught and held the gist of Jesus' teaching, and that gist is almost more than we can master.

One who ponders over these extraordinary passages is moved to speculation. What, really, is behind all this? Did Jesus actually say very much more than is set down in the books? Are these short graphic sentences and paragraphs the complete "word," or has much been lost through the summarizing of the first teachers and writers? Although it is quite clear that the earliest teachers, under the double compulsion of space and memory limitations, reduced longer speeches to short, swift, easily memorized forms, it is equally certain that *what* they report is the vital core of a message they could neither invent nor forget. They give us all that we can take or need. For example, what could be more probable than that the series of paradigms with which St. Matthew's "sermon" begins—the Beatitudes—are the recapitulating headlines of whole, separate discourses? And what could be less probable than the suggestion that such unutterable sublimity originated in the heads of some Palestinian peasants?

These, and many other sayings of Jesus, carry so

much force that, coming in direct succession, they
could not but distract and overwhelm the listeners.
Consequently, unless they actually were the starting
points of explanatory discussions, or their summations,
they must have been uttered, like proverbs, at widely
separated periods. But this last alternative is improbable. The simple members of His audiences scarcely
were more capable of grasping them in their existing
intensity than are the modern scholars who, despite
their erudition, find them difficult enough. Elabora-
tion was inevitable, whether in the form of longer
addresses, or by the ancient and more likely Socratic
method of question and answer. In any case these
precepts came with such beauty and power that they
were unforgettable, the vital core clinging to the
minds of the listeners long after the explanations were
forgotten. "Love your enemies. Bless them that persecute you." These explosives could not have stood
alone; nor could they have been diffused. We must
search, then, for the underlying meaning in the infinitely wider message of which the Sermon on the
Mount is but a part. It will be found in the revolutionary teaching about God and man that undergirds
the entire Christian Scriptures.

Are These Counsels Practicable?

Although the Sermon is anything but the heart and
soul of the Christian Faith, as has been pointed out,
nevertheless it is the very core of the ethic of our

Lord: the goal at which the believer aims as the ultimate pattern of his social behavior. Moreover, the
ethic is neither the beginning nor the whole of the
Christian life. It is an effect, not a cause. It always
must be understood as the gradually earned result of
that continuing spiritual experience which springs
directly, and only, from the disciple's personal relationship with Christ, the Lord and Master of the believing life. He is at once the Mediator between
penitent man and the Father; the Redeemer, whose
love compelled Him to give Himself for us; and He
who sends to us God the Holy Spirit.

Obviously, man is not "the Captain of his soul." As
long as he attempts to live by the dissolving promises
of that fatal delusion, he will be thwarted and defeated by the message of the Gospel. Even the
simplest of the counsels given on the mountain will
seem impenetrable links in a chain of steel. Yet it was
not for their ears alone that Christ said to those
Palestinian Jews, hard pressed by a legalistic religious
code too severe for the strength of any man, "My yoke
is easy and my burden is light." He was assuring them
(and us) that the main brunt of the battle is borne by
Him in a perfect alliance with all who believe. The
victory is God's, not ours. He is the Captain of our
souls, whose love will never let us go.

The standard set for all of Jesus' followers is high.
Christianity is not an easy, sentimental, childish faith.
Always it is hard going. Always it puts man's tenacity

of purpose to the severest testing. Always it demands
the utmost in loyalty, but never the impossible in perfection. Man is as a child in kindergarten, but the
immediate challenge is in accordance with his
strength. The goals, at first seemingly so far above
him, are reached through long processes of spiritual
illumination and moral growth. The seed of faith
grows secretly from small beginnings. The vision of
God becomes clear and yet more clear as the veils of
human pride, selfishness, and ignorance are lifted by
His increasing stature. The "impossible" becomes the
real.

Is this not what the greatest of all the disciples of
our Lord meant by the apparently difficult, but actually simple, doctrine of Justification by Faith? When
St. Paul says again and again, "You are justified by
faith," he is saying no more than that man's salvation
depends wholly upon the reality of his faith in the
God whom Christ reveals. He is assuring religiously
motivated people that their traditional meticulous submission to laws, rituals, and ceremonials (however
useful and beautiful) is as dust without this absolute controlling faith in Christ the Lord as the Redeemer King. "In him we live and move and have our
being" (Acts 17:28). That, to be sure, may involve a climactic change in one's outlook upon life: a
change of direction, a "turning," a conversion.

The crucial term *conversion* never can mean the

abrupt achievement of perfection. Certainly, the forgiven man is the commonplace of the Christian experience, but the sinless person exists only in the
fantasies of self-delusion. Yet conversion, a turning
around of one's habit of life, may be of dramatic
abruptness: a flashing vision of the reality of God in
which the sinfulness of the individual is revealed in
all its destroying detail. "Who will deliver me from
the body of this death?" Who, but Christ! Possibly
just this was the adventure of St. Paul on the road to
Damascus. Even so, it leaves us as we were, except
that it enables us to see ourselves as in truth we are.
This is not that seeing of ourselves as others see us—
a matter of no eternal consequence. Rather it is that
seeing ourselves in all our shocking sinfulness against
which is set in contrast the holiness of God. Yet for
most men conversion is a gradual process. The rusted
wheel is slow to move on its creaking axle.

When St. Paul, echoing the mind of Christ, made
the requirement of conversion clear, he also left no
doubt as to the sinfulness of even the greatest of the
saints. Men are leveled by the Gospel. The best of
them has not "already attained, nor is already perfect,"
but still pursues the distant goal of perfection, a goal
never to be won in this life on earth. And thus, although the sum-total of the ideas and the ideals of the
Sermon on the Mount is far beyond all possibility of
attainment by the secular man (the humanist, content

with the folly that the chief end of man is man), it stands as a challenging stimulant to those who have entered upon this alliance with Christ.

The new believer is not crushed by the dead weight of an impossible standard. He sees an end toward which he may hew out his path with the axe of faith. The ideals set before him are instruments to be used in the advance toward holiness; and holiness, the fruit of union with Christ, is the work of the Holy Spirit in possession of the hearts and minds of believing men.

But one must not think of *holiness* as a sort of super-goodness. Instead, it is a quality of personality reflecting the character of God, a state of life controlled by the consciousness of the reality and the presence of the Holy Spirit Himself. The word describes not what one does, but what one is. Here is no self-righteous contentment with progress; here is but a humbling acceptance of what it means to be the child of God. Holiness is a state of being in which the consciousness of sin finds its weight lifted in the exaltation of forgiveness.

Thus it will be seen that the Christian life is a life of grace. Although Christ, "the hound of Heaven," takes the initiative in calling men to His obedience and men must respond by an act of their own wills, daily faith and its issuing behavior are sustained by this influx of "power from on high."

But *grace* is infinitely more than the "favor" or

kindliness of God. It is the actual sharing of the divine life with man's life—the supreme gift of Christ to the disciple. It comes in a countless variety of ways: in answer to prayer, through the ordained channels of the historic sacraments, through meditation on the Holy Scriptures, in response to the thousand unspoken pleadings of the hungering hearts of men. Indeed, the dominant note of Christ's message is the utter accessibility of God. One need say no more than, "God be merciful to me, a sinner." And to that, when spoken in truth and penitence, comes the answer, "Son, thy sins are forgiven thee. Rise and walk!"

The Sermon Not a Model for Secular Society

From what has already been said, it should be clear that neither the Gospel of Christ as a whole nor the vital Sermon on the Mount is a possible ethical basis for a secular society. The principles common to all parts of the message must remain meaningless to the world of non-faith. Certainly, the secular population, at its higher and wiser levels, will admire the teachings of Jesus as the sublimest of all the systems of conduct ever offered to our dying race. But always this admiration is qualified by a wistful confession of man's inability to scale these heights: "It is a code for angels, not for the hard-bitten competitors in the struggle for existence." Of course, as we shall have occasion to see, certain precepts of the Sermon may have an expediential value for the secularist bent

upon the achievement of a particular purpose. Secularism, with the waning light of an ancient faith still
upon it, continues to find a practical social expediency
in an enforced obedience to sections of the Decalogue.
Murder, theft—now and then, adultery—still are
condemned by a society which, for the long moment,
finds their prohibition practical, though it has lost the
ultimate reason for their sinfulness.

Clearly enough, then, some of the injunctions of
the Gospel have a pragmatic worth-whileness. If tried,
"they work." But, in the long run, no social or philosophic pragmatism can be other than a transient expedient. It is action for the time, not for eternity. It
is concerned with today, not with tomorrow, and dies
at that instant when its ends are won. Its goals always
are set at a lower level than the aims of Christian
Faith. The aim of the righteous secularist, no doubt, is
a good and peaceful world in which to pursue his
materialistic, if ethical, ends. The aim of the disciple
is, on the other hand, the knowledge of God: itself
the purpose of the teaching of our Lord from its beginning to its end; itself the one means by which even
the secularist's dream can be transmuted into lasting
reality.

So the Divine Message can never be the model for
a worshipless ethical society, since secular man, devoid
of an ultimate allegiance to God, can have no goal
above his own selfishness. Always he is mastered by a
sheer expediency; and always expediency, variable as

the sand dunes, yields to new and vain ambitions in which ethical standards vanish as moral stability diminishes. In support of this argument one need look no further than the debating floor of the United Nations where, at the moment, the atheistic enemies of freedom flood the air with specious words timed to achieve a devilish pragmatic purpose of their own. And we, driven by a desperate necessity, are compelled to our own expedients. Expediency rules the realm of chaos. But Christ is the Lord of order, progress, and peace. Thus, we turn to the study of that which may be termed the rules of order for the progressive life of men and of nations—the rules and the keys of which the Church is the divinely instituted guardian.

Chapter II

THE BEATITUDES AND THE WOES

Matthew 5:1-12 and Luke 6:17-26

Should the reader of the parallel passages, Matthew
5:1-12 and Luke 6:17-26, be disturbed by the apparent discrepancy in both locale and content, he may
dismiss his doubts. Although St. Matthew pictures
Jesus as having spoken "on the mountain" and St.
Luke moves the event down to the plain, the general
position is the same. Obviously, the simple fact that
these compacted discourses were delivered over a
period of many days implies that Jesus moved about,
gathering the people of the clustered villages into
convenient groups at varied locations. Nor do differences in content pose a serious problem. The startling
condemnations of misthinking and misbehaving
which follow the Beatitudes in St. Luke suggest no
more than that, under the compulsion of personal
choice in selecting materials, he (or the author of his
source) considered these Woes too important to omit.
And the striking differences in parallel phrases may
be owing to the fact that St. Luke wrote much earlier.

He was closer to the actual events and probably more accurate in his quoting of their common sources.

Both St. Luke and St. Matthew used older written documents, and we shall find that changes in the life conditions of the Church made it essential that St. Matthew add certain explanatory words, not necessary when St. Luke was writing. Moreover, the latter wrote for Gentiles, while St. Matthew had Jews in mind. Their differences, however, are not vital. They serve only to exhibit the true power and diversity of the teaching of our Lord, as it seized upon the minds and hearts of His eager and often puzzled listeners.

The First Beatitude:
Luke 6:20 and Matthew 5:3

What did Jesus really say? Is St. Luke correct in reporting Him as having said simply, "Blessed are you poor, for yours is the kingdom of God"? Or is St. Matthew's, "Blessed are the poor in spirit, for theirs is the kingdom of heaven," closer to the mark?

The word *blessed* means infinitely more than a simple, transient earthly happiness. It implies a particular gift of the divine grace through which character is at once transformed and given spiritual sustenance. Only the word *joy* adequately describes the spiritual exultation that results from a conscious communion with the Eternal Source of life and hope. But can there be anything joyous about human physical

poverty with its rags, hunger, and inevitable sick-
ness? Is it morally possible to think of Jesus, with His
compassionate love for mankind, suggesting to families, shaking with cold and hunger, that they should be
content with their travail in the hope of an ultimate
blessedness on the other side of death? Could anything be quite so preposterous as the suggestion that
material poverty is either a required condition of the
good life or a necessary evil of the social order?
Though it is true that poverty, inflicted by a dis-
ordered social system or the sloth of men, may be
turned by strong characters into disciplinary purposes
as it illumines their understanding of their equally
stricken fellows, it has no standing in the Gospel of
Christ. For the moment Jesus accepts it, but never
does He bless it for its own bitter sake. Certainly, He
promises light and strength to the believing poor, even
as He impresses upon those who are materially more
fortunate the necessity of sharing their possessions
with the needy.

Since St. Luke's version of the Gospel is unques-
tionably far earlier than St. Matthew's, and probably
the original word of Jesus, we must press the issue.
What did Jesus mean when He promised His gifts of
grace to "you poor"? The answer is quite simple.

"The poor" long had been a technical term in the
speech of religious Judaism for the devout who endured unrighteous oppression, who spent themselves
to the utmost for the cause of truth and righteousness,

come what may. Naturally, inevitably, our Lord applied this term to His new disciples, upon whose shoulders rested the heroic task of establishing the Faith in a hostile world. They might have to become physically "poor for Christ's sake." Above all, they would, were the crusade of salvation to succeed, have to become so single-minded in pursuit of the goal assigned that every other interest would have to be cast aside. Pride, ambition, the love of power, the passion for popularity—all these would have to be abandoned in the pursuit of His purpose. Disciples must even be prepared, as one later put it, to "suffer unto blood." Since this is the background, we can understand why several years after St. Luke wrote, with thousands of Gentiles knowing nothing of Israel's struggles within the young Church, St. Matthew added the two explanatory words, *"in spirit,"* to Jesus' saying, "Blessed are the poor . . ." St. Matthew thus enabled non-Hebrew converts to understand more perfectly the meaning of the precept which undergirds the entire teaching and practice of the Christian life.

Nor is there any difference in meaning between St. Luke's and St. Matthew's expression of the promised reward. St. Luke's, "for yours is the kingdom of God," is today more decisive than St. Matthew's, "for theirs is the kingdom of heaven," because neither statement refers to the joyous rewards reserved for the faithful in the life of the world to come and because our Lord, speaking within the context of the complete Gospel, is referring to the establishment of the realm of God over the whole earth—precisely that for which, in a little while, He was to teach them to pray in the great "Our Father." The faithful would share the fruits of this victory over the embattled powers of evil. And, though this victory might neither come within the brief span of their earthly lives, as they had hoped, nor arrive by the means which they had expected, they were to learn through experience that conscious fellowship with Him is its own reward. That is the great compensation. "The poor" who shall inherit the Kingdom of God are those whose faithfulness has won for them the right to eternal life.

The Second Beatitude:
Luke 6:21 and Matthew 5:4

St. Luke's rough quotation, "Blessed are you that weep now, for you shall laugh," may grate on the ears of those who have learned the promise in the more sedate words of the Matthean report: "Blessed are those who mourn, for they shall be comforted." Yet the direct language of St. Luke is the very sort of thing that would have been said to crowds of beaten, thwarted people whose social, political, and personal sorrows had driven them to the verge of despair.

Jesus spoke not only to the believing multitudes of all the succeeding generations momentarily crushed by the shock of a loved one's death; He spoke also to the immediate contemporary group of oppressed Jews who, refusing to succumb to the horrid pressures brought upon free spirits by the ruling power, yet hoped for rescue and redemption. These people, as they listened to His message, could not grasp its profound spiritual meaning, but they could never forget the overwhelming personality who stood before them. And later, those among them who surrendered wholly to the Gospel proclaimed in the power of the Resurrection recalled His words and, in the recalling, realized the unspeakable joy that is the reward of faith. The Eternal Son of God, who had "humbled Himself" to become one with man in the full cycle of His being, tempted by all of man's temptations, suffering all of man's anguishes of body and of spirit in and through the valley of death itself, had risen from the very grave in conquest of that death. Now with irreducible certainty they knew that the full power and glory of the Godhead rested in Him. Now they were conscious of the fact that they, too, by the simple yet heroic act of faith in Him would inherit eternal life. To believe is to live! And so the sufferings, contingent upon existence in a world plagued and distorted by the sins of humanity in revolt against God, could be borne and overcome in the knowledge that the episode of "death" was but the opening of the doors into a wider, growing, and timeless life in the presence of the King, who is yet the great friend and companion of these who believe.

"Those who mourn" are not blessed by the inescapable experience of sorrow, though grief has its
disciplinary compensations. They "shall laugh" in the
utter joyousness of their victory over the temporary
sufferings of common life. And, when a believing dear
one is lifted across the invisible barrier called "dying,"
they shall be comforted by the certainty that the
separation is neither complete nor forever. For the
Church of God is *one,* and the spiritual fellowship
among those of us "on earth" and those in paradise is
real and endless. This we know even as we pray for
them, as they, indeed, intercede for us. This we shall
know in all the fullness of joy and its glory when,
with the barriers of sin, ignorance, and imperfection
overcome at our own death, we shall take their hands
in the presence of Christ. We need not speculate in
the folly of our ignorance. It is enough that Christ the
Lord, in the truth and power of His Resurrection,
should have given us the assurance of eternal life.
And, whatever the sorrow of our present lives, it is
enough that He should have said to us: "Blessed are
those who mourn, for they shall be comforted."

The Third Beatitude:
Matthew 5:5

St. Matthew alone remembers the saying, "Blessed
are the meek, for they shall inherit the earth"—almost
a direct quotation from Psalm 37:11 which reads,
"But the meek shall possess the land, and delight them-

selves in abundant prosperity." This apt use of the Hebrew Scriptures is so characteristic of Jesus' teaching method that no one is surprised by the thorough undergirding of His statements with principles already rooted in the faith of Israel. After all, the Church of Christ was not a new creation abruptly brought into being at the Feast of Pentecost. It was the old ecclesia of the Law and the Prophets, brought to its divinely intended fulfillment and clothed in the luminous garments of His perfect understanding. Only He knew the full meaning of the ancient faith, too often forgotten by its adherents. So every saying, lifted by Him from the historic Scriptures, assumes its true and final significance within the frame of the new revelation.

"Blessed are the meek," quotes St. Matthew, "for they shall inherit the earth." But, in the constant shift of word meanings with the changing generations, the term *meek* has been robbed of its original strength and beauty. In popular thinking *meekness* now suggests a cringing attitude, akin to fear; and "the meek man" is the last to whom we would look for leadership or the last we would trust with any task demanding courage, audacity, and self-control. Because of this, modern translators, notably James Moffatt, prefer to write, "Blessed are the gentle." Yet even *gentle* falls short. For now that our English speech has lost, perhaps forever, the significance held by the word *meek* for our seventeenth century ancestors who gave us the

King James Version, we can find no adequate substitute. We are compelled to resort to whole explanatory sentences.

Meekness, as used by our Lord, means an utter confidence in the purposes of God, a dependence upon Him so complete that every shadow of fear and uncertainty is swept away. This, indeed, is the aim of the believing life for which we must strive if the joy of spiritual peace and moral stability is to be ours. And, obviously, as our Lord utters it, the promise, "for they shall inherit the earth," has nothing to do with material power. He was thinking of the saint's true vision of God, which is the sole key to that peace that is of the mind and the heart.

Our Lord's understanding of the meaning of *meekness* powerfully illustrates the revolutionary character of His message. The psalmist, in saying that "the meek shall possess *the land,* and delight themselves in abundant prosperity" was thinking in the crass terms of a material wealth for the chosen people in their "promised land." His messiah was a triumphant second David who, if we for the moment follow the Authorized Version, would enable them to "delight themselves in the abundance of peace." But our Lord wipes all materialism from the slate of the disciples' minds. He speaks of a peace that has nothing to do with nationalist triumphs and racial messiahs. He proclaims the ultimate establishment of His Kingdom over all the earth—"provided we suffer with him in

order that we may also be glorified with him" (Rom.
8:17). The Cross of Christ avails for us only as we
are willing to share His sufferings in our dedication
to His service.

The Fourth Beatitude:
Matthew 5:6 and Luke 6:21

Again we note a striking difference between St.
Luke's report and that of St. Matthew. The latter,
writing with a longer, and perhaps deeper, experience
of the practice of the Faith behind him, modifies the
brief Lukan, "Blessed are you that hunger now, for
you shall be satisfied," by the qualification, "hunger
and thirst for righteousness." Certainly, the writer of
the first Gospel is fully justified in an explanatory
addition to what seems to have been the original
words Jesus spoke directly to a special group of cru-
saders "hungry for the Lord's sake." For, whatever the
technical meaning of "the poor," there can be no
doubt that actual hunger and thirst—the bitter fruits
of dire physical poverty issuing from persecution and
essential self-sacrifice—would be the sure experience
of many an adherent of the new Faith. Neither can
we question the certainty of both present and ultimate
spiritual satisfaction to those who, in any era, so suffer
for the cause of God and Truth.

The old Hebrew viewpoint, triumphantly proclaimed in Deuteronomy 8:10 and 11:15, promises to
the physically poor who do not waver in their devotion

to Jehovah a realistic material prosperity; and Isaiah
(65:13) holds, before the eyes of the faithful, future
spiritual joy and contentment. To be sure, the Prophets never restrict their visions of "good things to come"
to the lifetime of the contemporary community. They
look for the ultimate triumph of the Lord and His
righteousness over the existing forces of calamity
which, indeed, may be His chastisement of the nation
for its sins and its blindness. But the Bible is in spirit
a perfect unity which, studied as such, reveals to us
the ultimate purposes of God. These purposes, however feebly discerned by Prophet and Apostle, are
concerned wholly with the redemption of man, in-
extricably caught in the morass of the sins of selfishness and self-will. Perhaps only "a remnant shall
survive" the prevailing chaos, but it is to this remnant
that the Eternal Christ—whether in the voice of
Israel's prophets or in the voice of His new evangelists—speaks.

Our sense of the reality of the scriptural unity is
intensified in our Lord's correction and illumination
of the Law and the Prophets. He carries us into the
fulfillment of the Prophets' dreams. Thus, St. Matthew's words, whether our Lord's own or the author's
explanation, hew to the right line. Where the Old
Testament passages are occupied with the future re-
warding of a physical state faithfully endured, the
Gospel message introduces and stresses the necessity
of the pursuit of holiness for its own sake. Neither

physical hunger and thirst nor spiritual hunger and thirst possess virtue in themselves. The disciple must "hunger and thirst for righteousness." Not that he strives *only* for spiritual and moral growth within himself—a pietistic orgy that can result only in pharisaism—but that he must learn to lose himself in the passion to spread the good news of redemption to all men everywhere. Here is complete unselfishness. Here is the believer's realization in action that the business of evangelization is his personal business. To this end he was born, forgiven, and redeemed. On this purpose he must spend himself.

The Fifth Beatitude:
Matthew 5:7

"Blessed are the merciful, for they shall obtain mercy" must have come with some shock and surprise to a people reared in the primitive Mosaic law of "an eye for an eye and a tooth for a tooth." For, though the quality of mercy had long been stressed by the rabbis in synagog and Temple, it was more than difficult for the ordinary man to abruptly make so startling a personal revolution. "Vengeance is mine, I will repay" was then, as now, almost too much for the common man to take even from the mouth of God.

Genuine mercifulness, the inwardly compelled behavior of the balanced disciple, is tragically rare in a modern world schooled in the soul-destroying conflict of nations striving for survival. The very terrors of the early atomic era have encrusted us in hardness. The tensions of the hour—themselves the issue of un- certainty—have dulled our moral sense until we have come to accept as normal, thoughts and behaviors which would have shocked us immeasurably thirty years ago. It is not easy to be spiritually sensitive when the will, intellect, and heart of the surrounding world are united in a battle against a threatened tyranny. The very fear of the loss of freedom may steal that freedom from us; for in a war, whether of "nerves" or with the sword, liberty is stripped ruthlessly from either side. We have, willy-nilly, become the serfs of a machine. And even that compassion which once moved us to the care of the poor and the distressed has been taken from us by great, organized "charitable agencies" that accept our money in lieu of our hearts. The Good Samaritan did not hire an agent to be merciful on his behalf.

But mercy cannot be delegated. Despite the appall- ing pressures of the times, the disciple must never lose one iota of his compassion for the needs of others. Hatred, revenge, selfishness, must be torn out of his heart that mercifulness may take command. Here we are confronted with the judgment of God which re- minds us in unforgettable terms that the divine mercy will come to us in the end only if we ourselves are merciful in the present. Though later Judaism, its moral sensitivities dulled by persecution, may have lost something of this spirit, so essential to the win-

ning of eternal life, it was nonetheless part of the
ancient Deuteronomic code. The rabbis interpreted
Deuteronomy 13:18 in the words, "As long as thou
art merciful, the Merciful One will have mercy on
thee."

The Sixth Beatitude:
Matthew 5:8

In the sixth Beatitude, "Blessed are the pure in
heart, for they shall see God," there is, as usual, a vast
depth of Hebrew theology behind our Lord's words.
Without question, however, the contemporary application was intended as a constructive rebuke to those
who had mistaken ceremonial purity for the great
essential. That tendency, fatally typical of too many
modern "Christians," had been rebuked by the Prophets—"I will have mercy, and not sacrifice, saith the
Lord"—only to be forgotten when rites, ceremonies,
and sacrifices became ends in themselves. It is all too
easy to succumb to the corroding belief that decency
and respectability, sexual purity and social repute,
constitute the primary requisites of the believing life:
it is all too easy to imagine that a rigid or even a
reasonable adherence to the Christian ethic is all that
is required of a disciple. But nothing stands out from
the record of the "Good News of Jesus Christ the
Son of God" with more dramatic decisiveness than
the fact that the road of good behavior is not the high-
way to redemption.

Certainly, our Lord lays down for His followers a mode of conduct, a code of ethics. Certainly, the way to salvation is "a straight and narrow path." Certainly, the Gospel is intolerant of the impious belief, so characteristic of some oriental religions, that there is a complete separation between morals and faith: that it does not matter what one does with one's body, an insignificant lump of decaying flesh, so long as the soul sinks itself in the contemplation of "The Other." Certainly, too, Jesus shatters the complacency of externally ethical men with His bold reminder that the thwarted will to commit "sins of the flesh" is the equivalent of the reality. But here His concern spends itself on the vision of God as the road to redemption. For, whatever the satanic power of temptation, it is overcome by His response to the appeal of our faith. Again we see the profound significance of justification by faith, and again we are comforted and inspired by the sure knowledge of forgiveness. The black record of the past is not counted against us. It is the *now* that really matters.

Thus to be "pure in heart" is to give ourselves to an absolute singleness of purpose; to possess a controlling determination to pursue this end, come what may. Accordingly, it is the will that matters. It is our tenacity of purpose that counts, regardless of how often we may have fallen by the wayside. It is this passion of the heart, under the direction of the dedicated will, that clears away the mists that hide from us the face of God. If we so spend ourselves, He will reveal the vision of Himself to us and never will He let us go.

The Seventh Beatitude:
Matthew 5:9

The seventh Beatitude, "Blessed are the peacemakers, for they shall be called sons of God," has a particular pertinence to our bitter hour of human misbehavior. Our engulfment in sheer horror, as "nations rise against nations" and the whole basis of our civilization seems certain to be destroyed, has thrown us off balance. In increasing numbers, there is a flight from secularism to the Church as a last resort. Men and women, long separated from the Kingdom by their utter contentment with a godless way of life, are being driven by the terrors of the times to seek refuge in the body of the divine organism they long since have forgotten. The forgotten Christ suddenly becomes a last resort. And so, indeed, He is!

It is by the Lord's mercy that, regardless of our sinfulness, repentance alone will earn His forgiveness. Yet the meaning of His promise strikes into far greater depths. Jesus is not primarily concerned with the tragic incidence of "wars and rumors of war." Nations as such—their destinies, defeats, and victories— scarcely can be the business of a message that is occu-

pied with the destiny of man as man. The Good
News is the news that it is the individual who really
counts. Before Christ came preaching and healing,
man did not matter; he was the hapless tool of the
total state. After His coming, it was man, not the
state, who was of supreme significance. So Christ
speaks of peace of the soul, the inner peace which
"passes all understanding."

The peace that passes all understanding is not what
secular man means by "peace." Jesus deliberately divorces Himself from the always temporary panaceas
of the psychologist and the mental therapist as He
lifts us into a realm completely beyond the reach of
psychosomatic medicine. He is dealing not with
psyche, the life principle that none really can define,
but with *pneuma,* the spirit, which is wholly the gift
of God to His children "by adoption and grace." So,
in what are almost His last words, our Lord holds out
for the taking His offer of a new and different peace:
"Peace I leave with you, my peace I give unto you:
not as the world giveth, give I unto you" (John
14:27). This wonderful, indissoluble thing is the result of that knowledge of God which comes through
conversion and forgiveness. To know Christ is to be
possessed by His peace. To know Christ is to obey
Him. To obey Him is to extend oneself in "peace
making" everywhere. And this peace alone can overcome the evil that is in man.

The Eighth and Ninth Beatitudes: Matthew 5:10-12 and Luke 6:22-23

With the eighth Beatitude, St. Luke and St. Matthew again meet in quotation from the oldest written version of the words of Jesus; and, if their quotations differ slightly in form, it is St. Matthew who has done the modifying; the essential content and meaning, however, are the same.

St. Luke's source—obviously the report of an eye-witness—runs as follows:

Blessed are you when men hate you, and when they exclude you and revile you, and cast out your name as evil, on account of the Son of man! Rejoice in that day, and leap for joy, for behold, your reward is great in heaven; for so their fathers did to the prophets.

St. Matthew's verses are:

Blessed are those who are persecuted for righteousness' sake, for theirs is the kingdom of heaven.

Blessed are you when men revile you and persecute you and utter all kinds of evil against you falsely on my account. Rejoice and be glad, for your reward is great in heaven, for so men persecuted the prophets who were before you.

The ideas represented in these two parallel passages were addressed directly to the Twelve, training for their desperate, heroic task of evangelizing an antag-

onistic world. Certainly, St. Luke uses the same early
source-document that was in St. Matthew's hands.
Equally certainly, St. Matthew made important use of
another literary source and also felt compelled by
changes in the historical situation to modify the *form*
of the message to suit the somewhat changed conditions of his day. St. Matthew has historical perspective
in mind as well as evangelistic emergency. Persecution
has begun long since. To him it seems well that
people should know that they, like the first disciples,
are the objects of our Lord's warnings. They, too, will
suffer, and in that suffering they will share the divine
grace and eternal reward that was the lot of the first-
chosen martyrs for the Faith. Indeed, since they were
Jews, steeped in the story of their race, they had a
vivid consciousness of their spiritual kinship with the
Chosen People, whose remnant survived the horrid
chastisements of the Assyrian, Babylonian, Persian,
and Greek invasions. Now, it is *they* who are the
remnant! Now, in the refounded Church of God, it
is they who have become His special people, "chosen"
for the winning of mankind to the Messiah's revealed
Faith. And persecution at the hands of Antichrist will
be their certain fate.

Jesus' words are not given us simply for pious contemplation of the heroisms of our spiritual ancestors.
In them is warning, counsel, and promise to all the
generations of believers—perhaps especially to our
own. With the pressure of atheistic communism upon

us, we must not permit our fears to throw us off balance. The peacemakers who "shall be called the children of God" must be prepared for persecution—for scorn and ridicule and even expulsion from favored political, social, and religious groups—at the hands of those who regard Christian behavior in times of crisis as foolish and perhaps disloyal. They "shall say all manner of evil against you falsely, for my sake" has a vivid reference to the calumnious verbal assaults of moral cowards and ignorant self-seekers upon those who strive for peace through righteousness. The disciple holds no brief for that which the secularist mistakenly calls "practical," in the delusion that temporizing expedients will achieve the well-being of mankind. It is far, far better to be "expelled from their company," though that "company" be the congregation of a church, than to succumb to their misguided or evil will. But the hard words, "when men shall hate you," may be accepted as prophetic of those political powers of evil—first, the persecuting Roman Emperors and now, the persecuting States—which cannot exist unless they destroy every man's allegiance to Him whose authority transcends that of the noblest, as well as the most evil, State. For our age, atheistic communism may be the scourge, the flaming Antichrist bent upon destruction of truth, righteousness, faith—and liberty.

Our Lord makes it clear, in the verses before us, that mere resistance to the propaganda and the power of the anti-Christian forces abroad in the world is not enough, or even virtuous in itself. Men are "blessed" only when persecution falls upon them for the Son of Man's sake, for righteousness' sake. It is not enough to love freedom or justice or country for its own sake. One must love and obey Him from whom all these benedictions come. By direct inference, then, none of the ideals that we associate with democracy can have validity or long continued life in a secular society. Their whole meaning rests upon the degree that they are "in Christ."

The sentence, less extravagantly put in the Matthean version as "Rejoice and be glad, for your reward is great in heaven, for so men persecuted the prophets who were before you," does not mean that Christians are to rejoice despite their persecution. They are to rejoice because of it; not, of course, because of their suffering, but because of their ultimate reward in the presence of God. Through an unfailing devotion to their Christian vocation, they have won a redemption that cannot be taken away. Nor is there virtue or reward in self-sought martyrdom. He who is *thrown* to the lions is a martyr. He who *jumps* into the arena is a self-seeking egoist who "hath already his reward."

The Woes of Our Lord:
Luke 6:24-26

After the Beatitudes in St. Luke, there follows an amazing sequence of sentences which, in part, may have served as a foil to the blessedness promised to "ye poor," "ye that mourn," and "ye that hunger now." In the context of the Sermon, they are missing from St. Matthew, and yet they seem particularly apt at the point where St. Luke introduces them. Inasmuch as they come from the earliest strata of source material, there is no question about their validity, especially as they are fully congruous with the thought and the method of Jesus.

Immediately after Jesus' promise of eternal reward to the persecuted faithful, He says, "But woe to you that are rich, for you have received your consolation." Already we have seen how the "poor" are the recipients of Jesus' most profound sympathy—not that He ever attributes any virtue to the poverty which comes from either economic injustice or personal sloth, or that He condemns all wealth for its own sake. There can be a great compassion in the rich man's use of his possessions provided they are not evilly attained. Here His scorching excoriation of "you that are rich" is leveled at those who have found their complete satisfaction in the joy and power that may come from riches. They have already "received their consolation." They are content with themselves as they are. Not having sought out the knowledge of God, or having spent themselves in spreading the "evangel," they have not won the right to eternal life. They might, indeed, have "become poor for Christ's sake"; but in their freedom, they have chosen the selfish and the time-bound way of life.

The two following Woes constitute but a variant of the above principle. "Woe to you that are full now for you shall hunger" is a timely warning to those comfortable, contented, over-fed people who are pleased with their lot and find happiness in the sensual and the sensuous without resort to the spiritual. And "Woe to you that laugh now, for you shall mourn and weep" is leveled at the play-boy type who lacks sympathy for suffering people and has no passion for the service of God and the well-being of mankind. Jesus' warnings need not be stretched into an embracing of eternity. Their meaning is met to the full as one realizes the utter incapacity of pleasure seekers, whose sole resource is in themselves and their possessions, to realize the higher values of even ordinary life. With the mere mechanics of the sensual career stripped from them by economic depression or emotional terror, they flee from life through suicide. But Christ would redeem them and warns them in the only kind of language they can understand. It is significant that He does not hesitate to resort to fear when His diagnosis indicates its need. He is, indeed, the physician of the soul.

Following the Woes addressed to the wealthy and the pleasure seekers, there comes a striking warning against one of the most subtly destructive of all human weaknesses. Persons in high positions that involve some degree of power over others are particularly subject to it. Statesmen, lesser politicians, professional men, leaders in the business world, clergymen with followings of pious sycophants, labor leaders and beautiful women—all are the easy victims of a dread moral disease that issues in spiritual death through blindness. "Woe to you, when all men shall speak well of you, for so their fathers did to the false prophets."

Where this prevails there can be no real faith, no moral stability, and no genuine spiritual insight. Its victim has accommodated himself to the world and has become the slave of human convention. He does not what is right, but always what is "good form." He would rather offend God than violate the canons of that secular "good taste" which govern the class with which he runs. "What will people think?" is the standard by which this weakling governs his actions and his words, if not his thought. Of course, this mode of behavior becomes particularly sinful when disciples in positions of leadership in the Body of Christ become its victims. That men and women of wealth and social position should be shown favors not accorded to the faithful poor is akin to blasphemy on the part of human leaders in the Church. To them, as to their predecessors in Judaism in His day, our Lord said in unsparing language, "How can you believe, who receive glory from one another and do not seek the glory that comes from the only God?" (John

5:44.) What St. Peter calls "respect of persons" has no recognition in the Kingdom of God or in its earthly segment, the Church militant. The slave and his owner, the magdalene and the queen, the executive and the laborer are equal in stature before the Church of God. The measure of a man is his degree of penitence. Where faith is dead, there is no repentance.

It is inevitable that this controlling thought should immediately be carried forward in what is at once a promise and an injunction to the infant Church. The fact that the Matthean report omits the Woes in no sense breaks the continuity since this Gospel, at verse 13, stresses the incalculable significance of the Church to a self-doomed world:

"You are the salt of the earth; but if the salt has lost its taste, how can its saltness be restored? It is no longer good for anything except to be thrown out and trodden under foot by men" (Matt. 5:13). Or, as St. Luke gives it in another context—probably our Lord's separate repetition of the idea—"Salt is good; but if salt has lost its taste, how shall its saltness be restored? It is fit neither for the land nor for the dunghill; men throw it away. He who has ears to hear, let him hear!" (Luke 14:34).

Jesus, "knowing what was in man," sensed the anxiety and fear that must have overcome the disciples as He warned them of the rigors of the persecutions that would pursue both them and the Church until the end of time. Consequently, He tells them that the success of the mission committed to their hands depends upon their immovable devotion to His cause. But this is no promise of material security. This is a reminder of that fact that, as they set out to conquer the world for the Cross, they dare not lose the first freshness of their zeal. They must ever bear in mind the precepts that He has given them. Though they "suffer unto blood," they must repudiate all thought of compromise. To carry the flaming torch of light and life to the ends of the earth and to hand it on undimmed, though physical death be their reward, is their mission. The Christian, in this age as in the first century, is to be the "salt of the earth." He is to give to human society its tang of righteousness. He is to impregnate the entire fabric of man's world—its politics, its business, its labor, its professions, its international relationships—with the law and the spirit of the one message of salvation. To become weak, insipid, full of compromise is to have lost the savor of the Faith.

Never in history has the danger of compromising been so great and the temptation to soften down the message of the Christ been so strong. Seldom in history has the Church seemed so fearful of the meaning of its own commission. Rarely in history have appointed leaders of the evangel been so ready to remove from the salt of the Gospel its tang. Thus, no doubt, our Lord bypasses the failed leader in an appeal to the men and the women who are the separate seg-

ments of His Body that they may save it. Perhaps
(who knows?) Christianity will have to conquer
through the fearless evangelism of its nonprofessional
laity. But the Church, revived by the reconversion of
its people, is the divine instrument of redemption.
And so to the Church, Christ gives His challenge:
"Let your light so shine before men, that they may see
your good works and give glory to your Father who is
in heaven" (Matt. 5:16).[1] Here is an unmistakable
command, the divine imperative behind all the missionary effort of the Church, a moral parallel to the
great commission to "Go ye into all the world and
make disciples of every nation, baptizing them in the
name of the Father, the Son, and the Holy Spirit."

Missionary effort, however, means far more than
the support of consecrated missionaries by those who,
perforce, must stay at home. It means that every believing soul—the physician in his office, the typist at
her rattling desk, the dishwasher in the kitchen, the
man of business at his task—is dedicated to the same
cause. It means that every Christian, lest he lose his
savor, must in action and in word reveal the nature of
the Gospel as the controlling power in every aspect of
his life. The burden of the sublimest of all opportu-
nities is placed upon the Christian: he is a missionary.

[1] The preceding verse 15 has its sense included in this
summary.

Chapter III

THE LAW AND THE GOSPEL

Matthew 5:17-20 and Luke 16:17

Protestant sectarianism is still divided broadly into fundamentalist and modernist groups, and breaks yet again into segments that may be characterized by opposing attitudes toward the moral authority of the Bible and its spiritual interpretation. The Puritan heritage of some of the older sects has colored their traditional bibliolatry with an almost pharisaic legalism. Their morality is essentially that of the Old Testament and, therefore, largely negative in its popular presentation to a world which has ceased listening to Moses and the Prophets. On the other hand, there is a multiplicity of new-born sects with an impassioned "Jesus religion" which glibly assumes that the new revelation of the Lord once and for all swept out of existence the entire structure of the Mosaic law. To them the secret of redemption is to "believe in Jesus as Saviour and Lord."

To believe in Jesus as Saviour and Lord is, of course, a right conviction as far as it goes. But faith in

E. Eugene Poston, President

Gardner-Webb College

Boiling Springs, N. C.

our Lord involves infinitely more than an irreducible belief in His deity and redeeming power. It means, in addition, an acceptance of a divine authority embracing a particular ethic *plus* a theology of history.

To be sure, Jesus the Christ was neither a mere ethicist nor a professional theologian, but He did have a view of the full sweep of human history, and this finds expression in a speech which is in truth the language of theology. Jesus' is a theocratic universe. History moves under the hand of God. Events are not accidents. Events, the thoughts and the actions of men, issue either from the conflict between the free minds of rebellious men and the eternal purposes of God or, in fewer but notable instances, from the obedience of wiser men to the revealed will of the Father. But nothing is merely fortuitous—"God moves in a mysterious way, His wonders to perform." And the mystery is, in high measure, owing to human blindness, deliberately chosen. Sin is an attraction too strong for the self-willed. So God, permitting freedom, accepts a momentary thwarting of His purpose.

There is *a Christian view of history*: a view superimposed with an enlarging, interpreting intent upon the Hebrew concept of the meaning of history, a meaning that controls the whole literature of Israel. In the conflict between the forces of good and the forces of evil that at times seems about to engulf the Hebrews in chaos and destruction, Israel is certain of survival and ultimate victory. A remnant, the *ecclesia* of Isaiah, will survive and triumph in the end. Christ takes this for granted. And in the certainty of His conviction about Himself, He envisions His Church—refounded upon the Apostles and the Prophets—as the fulfillment of the purposes of God that had been manifested in the movement of Israel's life. The Chosen People, the people of God, have now become the Body of Christ. The process of redemption has become certain and quite clear in His Person and in His Word. All history is fulfilled in Him. All history finds its meaning in Him and His Gospel: a redeeming message which achieves its whole purpose in and through His Body, the Church.

Thus, probably because He had been falsely accused by the Pharisaic party, He vigorously announces:

Think not that I have come to abolish the law and the prophets; I have come not to abolish them, but to fulfil them. For truly, I say to you, till heaven and earth pass away, not an iota, not a dot, will pass from the law until all is accomplished. Whoever then relaxes one of the least of these commandments and teaches men so, shall be called least in the kingdom of heaven; but he who does them and teaches them shall be called great in the kingdom of heaven. For I tell you, unless your righteousness exceeds that of the scribes and Pharisees, you will never enter the kingdom of heaven.—Matthew 5:17-20.

The Lukan parallel simply enforces the identical principle. Together, these apparently distinct statements of our Lord make it clear that He accepted "the law and the prophets." But contingent passages, interpretations of specific Mosaic practices, exhibit His claimed authority to correct and to amend the old Law as part of the new turn that history has taken under His Person and His teaching. He gives new life and growth to the old Law which had become static. The divinely impelled movement of history compels new attitudes in accord with the purpose of God. And no one who reads will deny that in this action, climaxed by His death and Resurrection, He became the pivot around which time itself revolves.

The necessity of Jesus' position in relation to the Law is decisively clarified in the sentence, "For I tell you, unless your righteousness exceeds that of the scribes and Pharisees, you will never enter the kingdom of heaven." This was a blast against puritanism, and more. Orthodox Judaism had lost its spiritual vitality and its moral worth through succumbing to the fatal theology that salvation was to be achieved by a rigid obedience to the laws of Moses—split into a thousand meticulous applications by the lawyers and rabbis. Not only had the Law become an impossible burden of itself, but moral mechanization also had destroyed the believing spirit. Obedience had replaced action. Ceremonial and legal "sinlessness" had ousted love. Faithful Jews had come to think that a negative righteousness, a careful abstention from wrongdoing, was all that man needed for progress and redemption.

Our Lord, while upholding the necessity of obedience to the moral law, finds it impotent unless accompanied by the active rules of love in the free service of man for Christ's sake. Hence the Beatitudes correct in required action the negative social safeguards of the Ten Commandments. Hence the story of the Prodigal Son which, while showing the need of repentance, rebukes the pious self-righteousness of the elder brother who never having done wrong never has done good. Hence the parable of the Good Samaritan which makes active sacrificial love the necessary addition to quiescent obedience. Hence the tale of the Rich Young Ruler who "had great possessions." The man is halted in his progress toward the Kingdom of Heaven by his unreadiness to add charitableness at any cost to his respectable submission to the Law. And so it goes.

All this, of course, has a vivid application to the life of the modern world. These warnings are timeless. They are of the *now*. They tell us that the living Body of Christ in the world today may be thwarted in its fulfillment of the will of God by that contemporary pharisaism which blights so many Christian congregations: men who think that their full duty is discharged by financial support of the Church; women who substitute membership in societies (under ecclesiastical sanction) for the worship of God; persons who

devote their spare-time energies to ceremonial practices in comfortable churches; individuals to whom
social respectability and economic security automati-
cally win them a place in the Kingdom of our Lord;
others who trade upon their churchly ancestry and
find perfect satisfaction in themselves as they are!
Hence the Gospel's recording of that dramatic episode
of the once sinning women in the house of Simon the
Pharisee—"She shall be forgiven much, because she
loveth much."

In the background of Jesus' teaching, rests the sus-
taining truth that under the New Covenant, with
which our Lord modifies the Old, the Holy Spirit will
give to believing men the divine love that kindles and
upholds the love of the Christian for his fellow men.
This is the way to eternal life, to that "greatness" in
the Kingdom of Heaven promised by the King to His
loyal subjects. Yet, even as we rejoice in the new
Revelation, we must remember that it is *new* only in
the sense that it brings to fruition the Law that always
was valid for its times. It may be said that the Law as
it came into being was a concurrent integration with
the evolutionary process; that is to say, that God revealed the Law in such graduated stages as growing
men were capable of receiving. Sometimes man's freedom, abused by his ignorance and self-will, debased
the underlying ideal; but always the ideal was there,
and always the truth it held was the gift of God. Man
did not find Him. It was He who chose to speak to

Adam in the Garden (in a magnificant historic symbolism) as He revealed the price of freedom and the mode of rescue from its abuse.

Tribal patriarch and priest, tabernacle, synagog and Temple—in a grand evolutionary proceeding and itself the divine activity—exhibit the pattern that history has taken. That, of course, is the Church which Christ unites with Himself in and through His message and His Person. And redemption through the Church embraces in its sweep all who have followed faithfully since the day the Father cried first to erring man, "Adam, where art thou?" They too, those oldsters of the distances of antiquity whose loyalty wavered not, "shall be called great in the kingdom of heaven."

CHAPTER IV

SPECIFIC LAWS IN THE NEW LIGHT

Matthew 5:21-48

In contrast to modern writing, the Gospel narrative moves with an amazing swiftness. There is no waste of words, no attempt at artistry, as though the writers feared that any setting of the stage would only spoil the abrupt force of the message. Any conscious resetting of the sacred words is unimaginable. In the vivid memories of the witnesses, Jesus speaks for Himself so that nothing of the original flavor is lost. Unlike fiction writers, the authors of the Gospels were not inventing. They were recording truths and ideals utterly beyond the emotional powers, spiritual insights, and intellectual capacities of their own minds. In addition there is a startling difference between the literary prolixity of professional moralists and the sharp economy of Jesus' words. Having clarifed His position in decisive fashion, our Lord plunged into a striking exposition of selected examples of Mosaic "laws" that needed correction.

In addition to the examples that St. Matthew and

St. Luke preserve, Jesus, no doubt, actually modified or developed scores of other teachings occasioned by the eager questionings of the people; but the teachers behind the writers of the Gospel naturally chose to remember those which most clearly revealed His intent. These, on the whole, are specific rules of life designed to guide and to control the thought and the behavior of Christians-in-the-making, Christians surrounded and hard pressed by an indignant Judaism on the one hand and a morally corrupting paganism on the other. Like the Beatitudes, these are Church rules, a kind of primitive canon law, intended to preserve the integrity of The Way.

We must not think of the whole Sermon as an elaborated ethical code or as the complete moral teaching of Christ. It is at once a simplification of the vast, unwieldy mass of Jewish laws and a key to the future conduct of the disciples. Clearly it was Jesus' purpose to impress upon His followers the fact that, as against the old Law, His "yoke is easy" and His "burden is light." Yet this lessening of the load is never dependent upon the quality of the new revision. To live up to the standards of the Gospel is, indeed, a far more difficult task than was involved in the "righteousness of the scribes and Pharisees." But the "yoke is easy" and the "burden light" because its weight is shared by the Divine Companion. Any seeming unreasonableness in the demand is resolved in the fulfillment of the promise to send the Holy Spirit to the faithful.

And, though the gift of the Spirit was not (in the historical sequence) promised until later, it should be realized that the gift was already part of the full Gospel that the witnesses and the writers had received. We do not take the Sermon as set within the brief segment of its saying; we receive it within the frame of the finished message in which nothing stands alone.

Professor Frederick C. Grant, in his magnificently luminous book, *An Introduction to New Testament Thought,* expresses the oft-felt wonder of biblical readers at our Lord's apparent failure to condemn some specific evils as common then as now. It does, indeed, seem strange that we find no reference to such evils as gambling and alcoholism, vices which ate at the very heart of the ancient world. But this is not really strange in the light of the message concerning Himself. He does cite examples of objective sins—murder, theft, pride, adultery—through which His controlling principles found adequate illustration; but He could not—without contradicting all that was meant by His Incarnation—have condemned "things" as evil in themselves. Already, long before the whole record was written, heretical philosophers had risen who either denied the reality of matter or condemned it as intrinsically evil. "The flesh," they argued, "was evil"; hence the very manhood of Christ—"flesh of our flesh and bone of our bone"—could not have been actual. But our Lord would have none of this. To

Him nothing in all creation could by nature be evil. Only the thoughts and the actions of men could so be counted.

Yet Jesus does not evade the two instruments of sin, gambling and alcoholism, that have become so disturbingly significant in our day. With a hundred others He gathers the total treatment of the problem into the controlling principle of temperance. Men, using wine and food and money and pleasure, must never be misled into excess by inner weakness or outer temptation. They must be moderate. In short, with unfailing judgment, our Lord resolves the entire problem of the use of *all* things in the principle of *self-control*. He who is "temperate in all things" cannot fall by the wayside. Yet the believer is not always to be content with temperate behavior. There are times, as St. Paul points out to the Corinthian converts, when he must not only refrain from the mere appearance of evil, but when he must also abstain from innocent behavior lest he "cause a weaker brother to stumble." The Christian has a profound responsibility: he *is* his brother's keeper.

Thy Brother:
Matthew 5:21-26

Immediately after reminding His "students of The Way of life" that the gates of Heaven are barred against them unless their righteousness exceeds that of the scribes and Pharisees, Jesus sharply points to

His correction of the ancient social and religious tradition: "You have heard that it was said to the men of old, 'You shall not kill; and whoever kills shall be liable to judgment.' But I say to you that every one who is angry with his brother shall be liable to judgment; whoever insults his brother shall be liable to the council, and whoever says, 'You fool!' shall be liable to the hell of fire."

At once it is apparent that all sin has its origin in the will. Whether the issuing action is the result of deliberate intent or the wild fruit of the undisciplined temper, its origin is still in the will. Anger, uncontrolled, is itself that intemperance which results in murder, and he who gives way to it is a potential killer who cannot escape the judgment of God—although what that judgment may be we dare not say.

It is enough to remember that the justice of God is tempered by love, but not softened by sentiment. Of course we may say that there must be some difference between the punishment of the actual murderer whose cruel, hateful planning has achieved its purpose and that of the man whose exploding temper dissipates into sorrow. The God revealed in Christ is not a ruthless autocrat in whom compassion is always put aside in a strict exaction of the letter of the Law—nor would Christ have His followers degenerate into that impious, legalistic, condition. But He has no tolerance for the dangerous pretense that takes pride in weak outbursts of "temper," as though this

indiscipline were a virtue! And, if this violence issues
in insult, the judgment of the earthly court is as just
as the utimate punishment is certain. Yet "temper" is
a lesser sin than anger (unless it is its product) and
is disciplined accordingly.

In the King James Version the word *Raca* is left
untranslated, but it probably means empty head or
scamp. *You fool!*, a nasty, irritating epithet at its best,
was not regarded as serious enough for judgment by
the Sanhedrin; but because any belittling of the
sacredness of the human personality is completely
contrary to the dominant principle of Christian love,
our Lord declares that punishment hereafter will be
its reward. However, this is not to be understood as
having any relationship to the intolerable, eternal,
flaming hell pictured with an equality of sadism by
mediaeval monks and modern evangelists, a "hell"
whose literalism may be forgiven because of its ignorance.

In St. Matthew 5:23-26, there is an elaborate and
wholly Jewish illustration of a primary principle of
Christian conduct, as that conduct issues from the
intent of the will. One is reminded of a dozen references in the Scriptures to the priority of "mercy" over
"sacrifice." In these Matthean verses, Jesus used a familiar frame of reference to impress the disciples with
the truth that no material gift, no personal offering of
self or of possessions, is acceptable to God until one
has earned—whether or not he has received—the

forgiveness of those against whom he has sinned or held a grievance. Yet, in the dramatic and utterly human picture of first leaving the gift before the altar, drawn from contemporary Jewish life, Jesus presses home the practical necessity of "getting along" with one's neighbors even at the cost of sacrificing personal pride, which means so much and which gains so little —and that "little" utterly of this world. As a friend aptly says, "unless disputes with neighbors are settled, there comes a time when judgment begins . . . and the opportunity is then lost or, at least, considerably changed." Thus, as one follows the record, it becomes apparent that not only must the disciple seek forgiveness and reconciliation, but he must himself forgive.

A comparatively modern illustration of the Christian requirement of forgiveness and reconciliation may be found in the Book of Common Prayer, which forbids the reception of communion by anyone who has "done any wrong to his neighbours by word or deed . . . until he have openly declared himself to have truly repented . . ." (P.B., p. 85). That God forgives only the forgiving is one of the keynotes of the gospel of redemption. But the curious addition about escaping legal prosecution by making friends with the accuser does not belong here. (It is easy enough for a compiler to forget the exact source of a remembered saying that he wishes to quote.) St. Luke, in 12:58-59, expresses this concept in what seems to be its right context.

Adultery and Divorce:
Matthew 5:27-32

Precisely as the Fifth Commandment had its prohibition extended into the creative misdirection of the will, so the Seventh comes under correction. Jesus does not belittle the so-called sins of the flesh but, again and again, He reduces them to secondary significance as He lifts pride of heart and will to the throne of evil. By a strange irony, common debased human judgment has continued to resort to the ancient pre-Christian tradition which looked upon a wife as a bit of property: the most precious possession of the male, no doubt, but still a mere chattel. Hence this one-sided adultery was regarded by primitive men, whether of the tenth century B.C. or the nineteenth century A.D., as the defrauding of the husband of his rightful ownership. Adultery, in the Christian ethic by no means the worst of man's misbehaviors, is yet a sin, a cruel debasing of that singleness of the purposes of human love within the Covenant. Our Lord carries the implication further. Relentlessly pressing to the deepest roots of personality, once more He uncovers the real source of sin in the heart and the will of men: "But I say to you that every one who looks at a woman lustfully has already committed adultery with her in his heart" (Matt. 5:28).

The knife's deadly sharpness cuts both ways. In an age when the woman bore the brunt of man's one-sided laws, the disciple was compelled to the realization that the guilt was equal. If the Jewish legal atrocity that punished an adulteress with stoning to death had any validity, it must apply equally to the man whose victim she was: "Let him who is without sin . . . be the first to throw a stone at her" (John 8:7).

But our Lord is not driving furiously against the sin of adultery in a negative, puritanical fashion. Instead He is striving to develop within the consciousness of the believer such an all-possessing sense of purity that no room remains for the temptation to lust. "Who told thee that thou art naked?" is the query put through Adam to all men who look upon the physical beauty of the opposite sex only as an instrument designed for the contentment of an animal urge. This has nothing to do with the sacred relationship of the sexes temperately exercised within the marriage bond. It is a tragically mistaken interpretation which suggests that the Christian faith and ethic ever imputes the note of evil to the physical expression of love blessed in the sacrament of marriage.

Startling indeed, but completely symbolic, are the two sentences about plucking out the eye that offends and the cutting off of the member that is the instrument of sin! An even more dramatic presentation of the same idea is given in St. Mark's Gospel (9:43-45) wherein, as here, it quickly becomes obvious that Jesus is urging the tempted believer to undertake heroic self-disciplines designed to break the power of temptation. This means "avoiding occasions of sin," as teachers of morals put it—flights from temptation, if you will, when the strength to resist their pressure is lacking; hard disciplines which reduce their force, or drive it from the mind and heart; the absorption in concerns which lead the interests in other directions as new thoughts are built and habits formed. Although understanding the great Origen's fears, one can easily see his folly in mutilating himself while in terror of his normal sexual impulses. Scholars are agreed that our Lord in His injunctions against lust had no thought of the quite involuntary occurence of sexual impulses or of the unconscious striking of evil thoughts. Throughout His teaching, sin *always* is the deliberate action of the will.

When attention is focused on such passages as we have just studied, the problem of divorce and remarriage inevitably comes to mind. "It was also said, 'Whoever divorces his wife, let him give her a certificate of divorce.' But I say to you that every one who divorces his wife [except on the ground of unchastity], makes her an adulteress; and whoever marries a divorced woman commits adultery" (Matt. 5:31-32; author's brackets).

For all its sobriety of life and its magnificent social morality, later Judaism tolerated a pitifully easy divorce habit limited to the masculine sex. The new reformed Faith would have none of it. Our Lord gave

an unprecedented sanctity and an everlasting perma-
nence to true Christian marriage.

For the disciple the marriage relationship was terminable by death alone—a dramatic revolution in a
corroding civilization nurturing the seeds of its own
death in a hothouse of social immoralities. Sexual
promiscuousness, as prevelant then as now, had made
a mockery of marriage. With the family in swift
decay, the foundations of society were rotting out.
Drastic remedies were needed if man himself were
to hold his head long above the incoming tide of
sheer animalism. The empire felt these corrosives
gnawing at its vitals.

But Christianity was not concerned for the fate of
a nation as such. Its passion was to set up the "City
of God" in which men of all races might find rescue
and redemption from the common inner enemies. So
Christ, fulfilling the Mind of the Eternal, creates the
ideal of the indestructible oneness of the family. It
was heroic, magnificent, and practical. Society is not
to be saved by expedients; the dykes must top the
tides. Only the Church can recreate the broken unity
of life's basic institution.

We are not here concerned with the disciplinary
weaknesses of the later Church which, mistaking the
bracketed words, "except on the ground of unchas-
tity," for those of Christ, made adultery the prime
cause for the dissolution of a marriage. But neither St.
Mark (10:11-12) nor St. Luke (16:18) reports this

exception, and modern scholarship agrees that the words involved are a later addition to the text.

The text, indisputably repeating the actual words of our Lord, not only prohibits a new union with another on the part of one who has been divorced, but describes as adultery a single person's marriage to either of the divorced parties. This, of course, is the logical conclusion resulting from the absolute indissolubility of the Christian marriage despite the action of the State.

To be sure, conditions may arise within the married state which render its normal continuance impossible. Persistent, continuous adultery on the part of husband or wife (one being as bad as the other) would create such a condition and drive the parties into separation. Yet exceptional adultery, for all its nastiness and ensuing heartbreak, has been given a significance beyond its deserts by religious bodies and secular agencies unable to release themselves from either the cruel bondage of an ancient Hebrew heritage, on the one hand, or a pagan tradition, on the other. Indeed, this is a realm of bitter experience in which the believer may find the road to forgiveness hard or the life of separation a most painful discipline. But forgive he must; and should separation from "bed and board" occur, he must accept it. He has no choice but to master the virtue of self-denial.

Of course, this brief statement projects into the mind numerous questions that cannot be answered without a wide departure from the theme of this book. We may say, however, that, while our Lord forbids the dissolution of the Christian's marriage, His discipline is not applicable to non-disciples. Only Christians, baptized and so grafted into the Body of Christ, are capable of entering upon the Church's married life. Entering it rightly, and living through all its trials (some of them desperate!) in the spirit of their Lord, they will find marriage indestructible. It is a life of grace beyond the moral and spiritual capacities of the non-disciple.[1] What we cannot do by our human strength alone, we can do with the hand of Christ upon our wrist.

Oaths, Vengeance, and Love of Enemies: Matthew 5:33-48

At verses 33, 38, and 43 in Matthew we reach the high points of a trilogy of ascending difficulty in which the believer's heroism toward his fellow man finally meets its severest test. First, comes our Lord's comparatively simple modification of the ancient law of oaths before God. "Again you have heard that it was said to the men of old, 'You shall not swear falsely,

---

[1] The whole matter of *annulments*, wherein original unions are pronounced "null and void *ab initio*," should be looked into by puzzled readers. Sometimes these unions are invalid because they have not met the Christian requirement.

but shall perform to the Lord what you have sworn.' But I say to you, Do not swear at all . . ." (Matt. 5:33-34). This, of course, has nothing to do with the abominable and stupid habit of blasphemy through which many persons give vent either to their rage, their weakness, or to both. That folly is adequately dealt with in the Third Commandment, which makes blasphemy an absolute evil never to be mitigated by the self-condemning excuse of weakness provoked by the errors, failures, and misbehaviors of others.

In the verse before us, Jesus was concerned both with the old custom of binding every sort of promise with an oath before God and with a primitive lack of ethical judgment, the belief that such swearing were forever binding regardless of the nature of the oath. Certainly, neither solemn oath nor honest promise can hold any validity when contrary either to the will of God or to the well-being of man. But often an individual, pressed by moral tensions, may be unable to decide his course of action. His very conscience, the ultimate authority, may waver in uncertainty. In such situations our Lord counsels His disciples to avoid the difficulties by never committing themselves to more than a simple yes or no. Then, having disposed of the form of oath-making that might possess a legal authority, He launches into a swift discouragement of the popular Oriental habit of indiscriminately binding every slight promise and understanding by a variety of secondary swearings. Anything more, He warns them, is essentially evil. The full force of this is immediately apparent to anyone who has ever visited the Orient or grown familiar with the vocal habits of Orientals resident in the Western world. In a word, the believer will not swear by any of the Names of God or by that which is in any way associated with Him and His creation.

Obviously this confronts us with the problem of oaths exacted from men by the authority of the State. May Christians offer oaths of allegiance to nations? May they swear before the courts? May they pledge obedience to military superiors? To these questions there seems to be no absolute yes or no.

The laws by which men and States are governed must take cognizance of the existence of evil and, while the Quakers find strong support for their position in both the Scriptures and the traditions of the Church, it is by no means certain that our Lord forbids the oaths and the pledges normally required by the democratic State. Moreover, the early Christians solemnly bound themselves by oath not to commit any of the sins listed in the Decalogue or condemned by the Gospel. Again, in his magnificent letter to the early believers resident in Imperial Rome, St. Paul counsels loyalty to the powers that be: "Let every person be subject to the governing authorities. For there is no authority except from God, and those that exist have been instituted by God. . . . For rulers are not a terror to good conduct, but to bad" (Rom.

13:1-5). However, the subsequent story of the Church—in the stark tragedy of the early martyrdoms —exhibits in its most inescapable form the fact that times may come when the Christian must repudiate the State. None dare take oath to support an evil cause. None may dare for an instant to repudiate the dictates of a sure conscience at the command of Church or State or pure expediency. To find the current vindication of this truth, one need look no farther than the totalitarian countries of our contemporary world.

At Matthew 5:36 we are confronted with Jesus' final repudiation of the last remaining traces of the ancient law of blood revenge. In its primitive forms this practice, voracious in its vindictive destruction even of the relatives of those who had done injury to individual or family, was well-nigh limitless in its cruelties. The Old Testament, particularly in the books of Samuel and Kings, is replete with horrific accounts of blood revenge. So is the history of every race and nation from the dawn of history to the age in which we live. But, far back in the evolutionary process, these barbaric actions were the inevitable accompaniment of the struggle for survival. Men knew no more, and so could do no less. Hence the light of the Gospel exposes not their sin but their necessity, not their hatreds but their heroisms, as they battled for the right to a place in the sun. But our Lord is not speaking of that primitive unregulated social necessity of a forgotten savage past. He is dealing in a practical fashion with the later Jewish modification of the once uninhibited behavior pattern of the long-lost yester-days. Israel had outgrown its ruthless era. Israel's law-givers had rigidly regulated the old passion of blood revenge with the requirement that compensation balance the damage done. And so it was that "an eye for an eye, and a tooth for a tooth" became not only the law of Israel, but the actual foundation of our modern laws concerning the assessment of damages permitted by the courts.

But Jesus, speaking to a civilization which had long outgrown the barbaric social behavior of primitive times, strives to lead His followers to a yet higher level of faith and conduct. His disciples must repudiate even the legalized remnant of the days of vengeance. Yet, as He swept into the ash heaps of moral error the accepted legalism of "an eye for an eye, and a tooth for a tooth," He found Himself in opposition to the rabbinic school of Shammai which, with an incurable legalism, defied the evolutionary growth of the people and—insofar as Rome would permit—insisted upon the enforcement of a law already morally decadent. It was as though Hosea with his moving exposition of the final law of love had never lived! Our modern world, monstrous with its gadgets of destruction and flung backward into a well of darkness by the greeds and hates of a godless philosophy, is met by this evil of revenge on an unprecendented scale. So overwhelming are the tensions which have overtaken us that, as our animal passions rise in a surging flood, we are in the gravest danger of losing the primary ideals of the Faith. The counsels of St. Paul, written before the Gospels were set down and fully revealing the mind of the Lord, press hard upon our hearts: "Repay no one evil for evil, but take thought for what is noble in the sight of all. If possible, so far as it depends upon you, live peaceably with all. Beloved, never avenge yourselves, but leave it to the wrath of God; for it is written, 'Vengeance is mine, I will repay, says the Lord'" (Rom. 12:17-19). Thus one, having followed the life of Jesus, expects Him to amend the law of revenge: "But I say to you, Do not resist one who is evil" (Matt. 5:39).

The illustrations which fill out the paragraph (given also at Luke 6:29 ff.) are simple applications of the requirement that the disciple, emulating the love of Christ for all men, is to refrain from every trace of vindictiveness in thought and deed. Self-interest, the false concern of our economic and political life, is to be engulfed in the sacrificial motive governing a spiritual revolution. It demands, however, a heroism utterly beyond the powers of the pure secularist whose *end* is in himself. But Jesus, with an extraordinary insight that enabled Him to see "what was in man," anticipated a forthcoming conflict with rampant unbelief. "Turn to him the other cheek," "let him have your cloak also," "go with him two miles," and "refuse not him who would borrow from you"—all these precepts direct the behavior of the disciple in a hostile world. To survive and, surviving, to pursue ends as the evangelist of Christ, the disciple must at once be as "subtle as the serpent and gentle as the dove."

Implicit in Jesus' precepts is a shrewd bit of practical counseling, for martyrdom is never to be sought. It is to be accepted only when it may further the interests of the Kingdom of God. The Church, a vital segment of that Kingdom, must live if the purposes of God are to be accomplished. Thus, the persecutor should not needlessly be provoked. Yet in addition to "prudence," there is always a present pertinence to the counsels of our Lord. In them, is the standard of conduct for the day-by-day experiences of life. To "turn the other cheek" is an example of true humility—the "soft answer which turneth away wrath." To "let him have your cloak also" is a much needed reminder of the fundamental truth that, under the dire, unbalancing pressure of desperate need, theft—while remaining a crime—may cease to be a sin. (Meriting immediate forgiveness, it provokes a new generosity "because they have need.") And, "to refuse not him who would borrow from you" is a further expansion of the essential ideal of love in action. This is not indiscriminate charity by which sloth and fraud may be encouraged. This is compassion, a compassion never to be withheld lest we be "entertaining angels unaware." And such conduct involves that moral and spiritual heroism necessary to the subjugation of the sin of pride.

"You have heard that it was said, 'You shall love your neighbor and hate your enemy.' But I say to you, Love your enemies, and pray for those who persecute you, so that you may be sons of your Father who is in heaven . . ." (Matt. 5:43 ff). The tremendous implication of this counsel comes as a distinct shock to the modern reader who feels at once that he is far from the Kingdom of God. And, if such be his thought, he is right. The words of Jesus, except when He deliberately speaks in parables, are to be taken at their face value. Yet scholars may be right who say that this, like the preceding section, is an emergency counsel for a temporary situation and so not to be understood as a universal law for all the ages. Whether or not this is so, there is no room for dispute about the fact that Christ requires of His followers an exceptional degree of patience, humility and compassion without respect of persons. They are to be *a different people*.

The normal customs and traditions of human society run at a far lower level than that of the Christian standard. But never does Jesus exact of believing men that which is too much for their capacities, nor permit them to be tempted beyond their strength. To be sure, the Christian may be required by the pressure of circumstances to accept a degree of self-suppression above the ordinary! To be sure, there are times when he is compelled to submit to injustice, hatred, and

cruelty without complaint! To be sure, there is no
virtue in loving those who love us! But is not far too
much expected of us in this command to love our
enemies and to *"bless those who curse you, pray for
those who abuse you,"* as it runs in Luke (6:28)? In
a moment we shall see.

At long last the Church is learning to pray for the
enemies of those causes which the free nations es-
pouse. But too often such intercessions reek with a
self-righteousness quite as alien to the spirit of Christ
as are the deeds that are condemned. We must beware
of a soul destroying satisfaction with self, and nothing
can so assist the cure of it as the heroic self-discipline
of that love which issues in the selfless prayer for the
spiritual well-being of "them that hate us."

Although the over-all command of Jesus controls
our attitude toward those national groups of enemies
whose espousal of evil appalls the free world, in the
counsel to "love your enemies," He is speaking about
the attitude of the individual toward those whom he
regards as his personal foes. Curiously enough, the
Mosaic law that commanded men to love their neighbors nowhere suggested the hate of enemies. That was
simply a logical assumption which, considering human nature, was read into the old Law. Yet if love be
the deep passion of the heart of man, if love be that
emotion which moves between the mother and her
child, if love be that inexplicable feeling which

blindly binds the hearts of sweethearts into one consuming purpose, then Jesus' message is but the folly of a hopeless dreamer. Man cannot, even if he dared, love his enemies; though in his last hours he may, with Christ, forgive them their wrongs against him.

Yet here is a satisfying explanation of this apparent anomaly within the very language itself, in the Greek on which our English translation is based. That amazingly mobile tongue, with its flair for terms which interpret the full play of the mind and the emotions, has several words for which our rugged English can find but one unsatistfying translation. Among the Greek terms that we translate by the word "love" is the word *eros*, the flaming sensual passion of the sheiks of Araby, the love that so often consumes itself in lust. Another is *agápê*, the term used with great precision by St. Paul in the moving hymn to Love in I Corinthians 13. *Agápê* was a word deliberately chosen by the teachers of the Gospel because it was completely dissociated from the corrupting lust eating out the heart of Roman civilization. The term had so fallen into disuse that it is difficult to find *agápê* employed in the Greek writings of the day, although the Hellenistic Jews had it in their Greek Old Testaments. It means a spiritual compassion for men that causes all their actions to hew to the line of justice and fair play. To read St. Paul's exposition of its meaning in thought and in action is to discover that to "love your enemies and pray for those who persecute you" is, after all, the difficult, heroic, yet practical rule of the life of grace.

St. Matthew's fifth chapter ends with the words, "You therefore, must be perfect, as your heavenly Father is perfect" (5:48). It is, I think, one of the original series of addresses from which the Sermon on the Mount was constructed. It is a hard saying, an impossible ideal—but only when considered from the standards of a mundane, swiftly terminable life. It is not an injunction meant to be fulfilled within the short embrace of threescore years and ten. Rather, it suggests a process wholly integrated with the quality of that eternal life which begins for the faithful here and now. Conversion is the birth into the life eternal. Perfection is the goal to be won through the timeless process of growth into the likeness of Christ, not here on earth alone, but here and hereafter. It is in the life of the world to come that the goal posts stand.

CHAPTER V

THE FLAME OF LIFE

Matthew 6:1-34

Although it is quite certain that Jesus espoused neither a political ideology nor an economic way of life, it is equally clear that He laid down a specific pattern of principles by which the leaders of men must cut their cloth. There is no *Christian economics,* despite the passion of some reactionaries to bend the Gospel into the narrow shape of their partisan belief. Yet there are political and economic practices for which the Gospel of redemption can have no tolerance, since they contravene the laws of behavior that bind the disciple and the Church of which he is a part. Within the binding fabric of the Gospel, there is a perfect integration of the individual with the Body of Christ.

The principle which governs the individual in his relationship with his fellows controls the Church of God in all her corporate thought and action. This follows because, throughout the Sermon, Jesus describes the individual as he reflects and interprets the mind of the Church whose Head is Himself. The New

Israel is the divine instrument for the projection of
the will of God into the full sweep of human life; and
it is the business of its members to fulfill in action the
truth that all is His and nothing man's. Hence no
sphere of life can ever be isolated; for man is one, and
in that oneness he is wholly subject to the mastery of
the King. Thus the function of the Church carries her
into all the thoughts, dreams, and actions of her children.

The precepts enunciated in Chapter IV render political and economic isolationism on the part of men
and nations morally impossible. The neighbor whom
the believer must love ceases to be the man next door,
for in the vision of the Christ, he becomes the "enemy" with whom that love is to be shared. In similar
fashion, each of the principles laid upon the disciples
in training is to become the guide of groups and nations in all their dealings with their kind until,
through the devotion of our action, the mercy of God
dissolves the nations into the single family of Christ.
That day may be so distant that its coming seems to
matter little to us. Yet the disruption of the nations
continuing before our very eyes suggests that it may
be far closer than we know. But speculation is futile,
dangerous, and blind.

From the precepts governing man's behavior toward
man, our Lord turns next, according to St. Matthew's
report in his sixth chapter, to the consideration of the
disciple's attitude toward God. In doing so, He shows

the disciple how to kindle the flame of life that will light the pathway to his goal.

A Key to Devotion:
Matthew 6:1-7

Ostentation, itself the result of pride, is a trap ever lying open for the religiously minded, especially for those who find satisfaction in the practice of humility. The good man does not "wear his religion on his sleeve" or parade the evidence of his holy zeal before the eyes of men. Humility is that virtue of which the possessor is least aware and which pride most often imitates. That this is an ever-present danger to the well-being of the soul is stated decisively by our Lord as a necessary preface to His discussion of the spiritual life: "Beware of practicing your piety before men in order to be seen of them; for then you will have no reward from your Father who is in heaven" (Matt. 6:1). The Christian's devotions, including his charitable acts, are for the ears and eyes of God alone; and he will constantly avoid actions done with even the admirable desire of "setting an example" to the ignorant. That which he must do in public will always be done with the selfless motive that characterizes the secret prayers of his loneliness.

Jesus dramatizes the point with an illustration drawn from a practice tragically common in this our day when the impoverished Church, driven to highly advertised campaigns for the furtherance of the Gospel, appeals to rich and poor alike for financial support. Always there are persons whose giving to "good causes" is mothered by the hope that the trumpets will sound in thanksgiving for their generosity or that they will receive, at least, a humbler credit for their deed. Always there are leaders who, in a peculiar blindness to the implications of our Lord, extravagantly praise these individuals before their fellows. Yet the expression of thankfulness cannot be withheld when it is due, but it is due only when the act exceeds the requirements of duty. Hence the disciple must keep an exacting watch upon his motives. He may be pleased by the gratitude that others express, but the moment he expects it, that is the beginning of his downfall. "Truly," says Jesus of such men, "they have their reward" in the transient satisfaction of the prideful moment. But the Christian building the temple of eternal life has but one mode of action: "When you give alms, let not your left hand know what your right hand is doing, so that your alms may be in secret; and your Father who sees in secret will reward you" (Matt. 6:3-4). Nor is this a reward to be given only in the life of the world to come when the believer attains perfection. It comes here and now in the stabilizing and illumination of spiritual character.

Then, just as the believer may claim no earthly credit for his giving—least of all bring no pressures to bear because of it—neither may he accept the praises of men for the piety of his life. Jesus stamps with the burning brand of hypocrisy those who make a public display of their prayers. That momentary admiration of the misguided will be their sole reward. *"But when you pray, go into your room and shut the door and pray to your Father who is in secret; and your Father who sees in secret will reward you."* Once more, as always, it is the motive that matters. Not for an instant is Jesus condemning the public prayer, liturgical and individual, that was the habit of His own earthly life. What He condemns is a display, with hope of praise, that is its own reward.

In addition to the obvious impiety of those who pray "to be seen of men," there is another peril to spiritual integrity, so subtly concealed that often it is missed. It is to be seen in the tendency of devout men and women to freely talk about the inner experiences incident to their own life of prayer—how often they pray, the hard discipline which they inflict upon themselves, the number of persons for whom they intercede, how God rewards the intercessions of their hearts! And again we see the manifestation of the sin of pride in its most dangerous form; a form none the less perilous because it is often unconscious. The individual, lest he "have his reward" in the admiration of his disciples, never may make himself the model for his teaching; nor in his public nonliturgical intercessions must he yield to the temptation to be eloquent, heaping up "empty phrases as the Gentiles do; for they think that they will be heard for their many words." With unconscious irony, a recent press release about the author of a book of prayers said, "The chamber was always crowded by senators eager to hear his beautiful prayers." Still, it is true that now and then there have been saints who could freely talk about the experiences of their inner lives completely without self-consciousness and pride. Still, it is true that you and I are not likely to be among them. The saint never is aware of his saintliness.

Prayer and the Model Prayer: Matthew 6:9-14 and Luke 2:2-4

That there never has been a soul who did not have some trouble with his prayers is comfortingly recognized by our Lord. No sooner has He finished His strong yet gentle castigations of the exhibitionist Gentiles than He says, "Do not be like them, for your Father knows what you need before you ask him." Today there is much concern about words and forms and techniques. Even preachers and teachers who ought to know better constantly discourage simple people by dwelling upon what they call "the difficulties of real prayer"—as though God were a pompous business executive with a dozen secretaries to be bypassed before one may catch His hard-pressed ear!

There are, of course, valuable techniques to be mastered by those of us who would scale the heights of the spiritual life, techniques in which the great saints have always been at home. And there are simpler

methods to be learned by us whose attempts to pray
are harried by personal weaknesses: the inability to
concentrate, the wandering of our mind, the apparent
coldness of our feelings. Even Saint Teresa battled for
seventeen years with these commonplace troublings
of the sincere heart; and once I heard the late Bishop
Winnington-Ingram of London say, "Last night I had
to begin the Lord's Prayer over again no less than eight-
een times before I could finish it without alien
thoughts creeping in." It becomes clear, then, that
these techniques in no way govern our actual approach to Him. They are methods designed to help
us through difficulties created by our own weaknesses.
Even so they are greatly overstressed. Before all else
we need to know the utter accessibility of God. He is
our Father. His very heartbeat is tuned even to our
unspoken need. His answer is to the cry of our hungry, anxious hearts rather than to the eloquence of
our lips or the discipline of our minds. His one
requirement of us is the will to approach Him. As
free beings the initiative here rests with us. He knows,
but He cannot answer until we speak—though it be
with but the yearning of our spirits. Thus, in giving
to the disciples the primary model of all prayer, He
says very simply, "Pray then like this:"

> Our Father who art in heaven,
> Hallowed be thy name.

Strange as it may seem, neither the words of our
Lord nor the rest of the New Testament has much

to say about the brotherhood of man. The whole basic law of life rises out of faith in the Fatherhood of God. Brotherhood has no meaning to the inhabitants of a godless world except as a fading hangover from an ancestral conviction of the reality of God and the necessity of man's devotion to Him. Thus we are told to say always "Our Father"; and, lest we lose sight of the transcendence of God (the fact that He is a person quite other than the universe that is His handiwork) and sink into that utterly hopeless pantheism which would see Him in everything and everything in Him, we are reminded in every prayer that He is "in heaven." Man is not a part of God, a helpless cell in a mighty seething mass of pointless life of which the Deity is the sum total.

The unfailing ascription, "Hallowed be thy name," isolates the Divine Personality in an unutterable holiness. He is never to be approached except through the mood of reverential awe—the Absolute, the Alone, the Person who is the Creator and Master of all persons, yet whose love turns His very holiness to the service of His children. Inevitably, then, the believer never can make light use of the sacred Name that represents all that God can mean to man, and infinitely more.

> Thy kingdom come,
> Thy will be done,
>   On earth as it is in heaven.

"Thy kingdom come . . ." is the confident cry of one who knows that he will share in the ultimate triumph of the victorious Christ. Certainly, the rule of God is to come about as men allow Him to take possession of their minds and hearts. Certainly, the Kingdom can come to full flower only as men do perfectly on this earth the divine will as it is done in heaven. And men must ever pray and work that this may come to pass, as in some slight measure it does whenever individuals and groups pledge themselves to the service of the King. Yet there is another note ringing through this prayer, one that sounds throughout the entire Gospel of our God. One hears it take its rise in the Old Testament's portrayal of Israel's story; one hears its volume increase until in the Apocalypse of St. John the Divine it bursts forth in a final crescendo. Though the faithful, in the terrible battle between good and evil, between truth and falsehood, between God and Satan, may be reduced to a remnant, God is not to be defeated. In this prayer we cry out to Him to "take up Thy power and reign," and He will not be found wanting. But the words, "Thy will be done," also imply a primary discipline essential in all of man's relationships with God. The complete activity of the Christian is governed by his consciousness that nothing is to be thought or said or done unless it is in accord with the will of God. Yet, since the human conscience is never perfect and the individual is often thrown into uncertainty by un-looked for situations, this principle must control the prayer which precedes our thinkings and our doings. The wisest and holiest of men cannot be sure of the ultimate rightness of the course before him. So every prayer, regardless of its purpose, is offered in the con-viction that its answer is wholly dependent on its conformity to the purposes of God: "Not my will, but thine be done, O Lord!"

Abruptly, the great model prayer turns to what at first thought seems to be a strangely mundane inter-cession. We are dropped, as it were, from the holiness of heaven into the stark struggle of the earthy life. Yet the psalmist should have prepared us for this by his familiar cry, "The earth is the Lord's, and the full-ness thereof." After all, despite secular man's forget-fulness, the primary eternal oneness of creation as the handiwork of God is a profound and basic prin-ciple of all theistic faith. That language which speaks of "the secular" and "the sacred" as different or con-trary spheres of existence is at once biological, social, and religious nonsense. Man is one. He is the child of God. The full movement of his life is integrated with his faith and his worship. He sings his hymns, digs his ditches, bakes his bread, and plays his games—all to the glory of God. Thus his intercessions embrace the broad, inclusive sweeps of his activity, and so he must say,

Give us this day our daily bread.

The precise meaning of "Give us this day our daily bread" is touched with uncertainty. The best translations put in their notes "Or, our bread for the morrow"; and this seems to be more accurate. The disciple, content with the supply of physical needs for the day —enough to have enabled him to do the work of God —intercedes for the well-being of the believing community. For himself he asks nothing that he does not ask for others. Unlike many modern prayer books and teachers of the modes of the devout life, Jesus steers us away from what a deep-seeing friend of mine ironically calls "especially prayers." Never, never are we to single out individuals, congregations, nations, or ourselves for the special favor of the Lord. Neither Englishmen nor Americans nor Chinese are the favorites of the Father of us all. All needs are alike, and all alike need the forgiveness of our Saviour.

And forgive us our debts,
As we also have forgiven our debtors;

"And forgive us our debts . . ." is "a hard saying"; a requirement utterly beyond the capacity of one who has not made his peace with God by the forgiveness of those who have sinned against him. "Debts," "trespasses," "sins"—these all are variants of the same term. Our Lord is speaking bluntly of the inescapable necessity of our complete forgiveness of others before we dare intercede with Him for the forgiveness of our own sins. "For if you forgive men their trespasses, your heavenly Father also will forgive you; but if you do not forgive men their trespasses, neither will your Father forgive your trespasses" (Matt. 6:14-15).

In Chapter IV we said enough about sin as "that which separates from God." Here we need do no more than stress the fact that the individual sinner's reconciliation with God is to be achieved only through that measure of his love which, expelling hate, forgives if it does not forget the wrongs done him by others. In short, He deals with us as we have dealt with others. Thus, as we pray for forgiveness, we are really praying for the will to conform ourselves to the purposes of God and to be "one with Him as He would be one with us." Certainly this is one of the most difficult of all the ways of thought and behavior expected of us, and yet nothing is more practical. If men everywhere can be brought through faith to say with absolute devotion, "Thy will, not mine, be done," the peace which is the prelude to the coming of the Kingdom will be at hand, and God will reign.

> And lead us not into temptation,
> But deliver us from evil.

Old-fashioned commentators, deeply rooted in the Puritan tradition with its heavy emphasis on Old Testament teaching, used to teach the intolerable doctrine that God Himself deliberately tempted men in order to test their powers of resistance and thereby develop character. To be sure, there is a high degree of truth in the claims that temptation *resisted* develops strength and that, while the Father never tempts men to sin, He permits it. But He allows it not for any such salutary purpose as the building of character. He allows it because in the divine economy, whereby He sacrifices His own power that man may be free, He cannot help it. Thus temptation is the price that man pays for freedom, and sin is the price that God pays for the offering of His love—a price which was once and for all met to the full in the agony of Calvary.

In the phrase, "lead us not into temptation," we really say, "let not the strain of our temptations be too much for our strength." And in reading it, we recall that Christ Himself entered so completely into our humanity that He was "tempted in every respect as we are" and, with no strength beyond that available to us, remained "without sin" (Heb. 4:15). Temptation will beat incessantly upon us, rising, as St. James says, "out of our own desire" (1:14), but—no sin in itself—it can be rejected by the grace of God. It is for that grace that we pray.

Interestingly enough the second clause, "But deliver us from evil," may be read as *"deliver us from the Evil One."* This comes from ancient Hebrew sources in which *yetzer ha-ra'*, the evil disposition or tend-

ency, is identified with Satan and with the Angel of
Death. This, of course, is a typical primitive personi-
fication of evil and death—"the soul that sinneth, it
shall die"—rising out of the basic story of the Garden
of Eden in which Adam's sin was the cause of man's
dying. But the reality is unchanged and unchanging.
Man, with the prize of liberty his dearest possession,
is confronted with a momentous challenge at every
instant of his career. He must choose either life or
evil, either Christ or death. "As in Adam all die, so
in Christ shall all be made alive" is St. Paul's magnificent compaction of this profound theology. The
lesson of Genesis is the message of Christ and the
Faith of the Church. So, in effect, we pray, "deliver
us from the evil which leads to spiritual death," a
plea for power to so resist the corroding effects of the
willfulness of sin that we may win eternal life. In the
last analysis we throw ourselves completely upon the
forgiving mercy of our God.

At this point the Lord's prayer abruptly ends. There
is no more to be said. We have made our choice between death and life. Our apprehension that something is missing comes from our familiarity with the
grandeur of the King James Version in which, as in
the historic liturgies, the joy of the forgiven believer
bursts from its restraints into a magnificent doxology—

> For thine is the Kingdom, and the Power, and
> The Glory, forever and ever. Amen.

This doxology, a brief yet complete hymn of praise, is not to be found in the best of the modern translations simply because it does not appear in any of the more ancient manuscripts. The words are not the utterance of Jesus. Instead they are the united response of early Christians as they participated in the corporate adoration of the New Israel; they were part of the liturgical setting in which the Sermon on the Mount was cast for the worship of the fellowship. Scarcely could there be a more thrilling climax than this shout of praise, this ascription of all power and glory to the Eternal Redeemer King! And today we say and sing it, reflecting in our action the devotion of the Body of Christ in Upper Room and catacomb, in little country church and great cathedral. This, indeed, was the kindling of the flame of life that neither man nor devil can extinguish.

Some Further Personal Counsels: Matthew 6:16-34

We need not quote the significant directions concerning the Christian method of *fasting* as part of the fellowship of prayer given so clearly in Matthew 6:16-18. Perhaps those scholars are correct who say that in the actual utterance of our Lord these sentences immediately followed the earlier excoriations of those Gentiles who "prayed to be seen of men." Nevertheless they are singularly pertinent here; for *fasting*, the traditional concomitant of prayer, uniquely lends

itself to that disastrous ostentation which so easily
intrudes itself into scenes of corporate intercession.
"The hypocrites," professing humility, took then, as
they take now, a strange delight in the publicising of
their devotional life. Their contemporary counterpart
is to be seen in those individuals who publicly proclaim their utter devotion, despite the sacrifice, to
their church's rules of fasting and abstinence—"as an
example." But genuine fasting, clearly enough a
prescription of our Lord for His followers, is to be
done always in utter secrecy. None is to know of it
by any outward sign, whether of appearance or of
word. It is a secret compact between the man and His
Lord, a part of that essential discipline of all the
physical desires and appetites, commonly called "temperance," which develops moral strength and spiritual
insight. It is also and importantly a part of the volun-
tary sacrifice through which one shares in slight
degree the sufferings of Christ "for us men and for
our salvation." And that, surely, is reward enough
for the cheerfulness characteristic of the true believer.

The remnant of St. Matthew's sixth chapter, run-
ning from verse 19 through verse 34, should be considered as a whole. Although it appears to deal with
a number of separate ideas, these are but effectual
illustrations of the common theme that underlies not
only the Sermon but the whole of the Gospel. This is
the necessity of an irreducible singleness of heart.
One will, one all-possessing purpose, drives the Chris-

tian to his goal. Nothing, whatever its seeming worth, can be allowed to turn him aside from his devotion to the purposes of God. He must be "poor for Christ's sake." But, as we pointed out in an earlier chapter,[1] the words, "Do not lay up for yourselves treasures upon earth . . ." have no direct bearing upon the mere possession of material wealth, neither do they bless physical poverty, as though to exist always on the verge of starvation were a virtue.

Our Lord is driving hard against that avarice which, once material wealth becomes in itself the dominant concern of one's existence, expels every interest in both cultural and spiritual realities. Always this covetousness creates an anxiety which diverts its victim from the stabilizing illuminants of the spiritual life, ruins his worth to society, and dulls his normal human perceptions. Ironically enough, more often than not, it defeats its own selfish purposes because the man becomes more and more immersed in a process that will not let him go until old age compels him to retirement—and then he finds himself ignorant of both the things of men and the things of God. This bitter state is dramatically and sadly exposed in the story of the Rich Young Ruler who, wanting to follow Christ, found himself already the slave of his possessions. The position is brought to a sharp focus in words that seem almost obvious—"for where your

[1] See comment in Chapter II on Matthew 5:3 and its Lukan parallel.

treasure is, there will your heart be also" (Matt. 6: 21). The Christian must make the pursuit of the knowledge of God his present and his ultimate objective lest he lose it altogether. Singleness of purpose and unworldliness—these must be his commanding objectives come what may!

Verses 22 and 23 amplify the position. "The eye is the lamp of the body. So, if your eye is sound, your whole body will be full of light." With one's sights fixed upon the vision of God, there can be no diversion of the will into secondary channels except insofar as these are aids to the achievement of one's purpose. And when Jesus warns that "if your eye is not sound, your whole body will be full of darkness," He means not simply "the deceitfulness of riches," the trap into which pride invariably leads, but the entire field of man's ambitions and desires to the control of which he all too easily subjects himself. To be the greatest singer, the greatest artist, the greatest preacher, the greatest scientist in all the world, the greatest . . . ! These are evidences of the unsound eye through which the "whole body will be full of darkness," unless these skills are made the instruments through which one's singleness of purpose gives glory to God. Friar Juniper, humbly cooking in the hot kitchen of the monastery, responds to the sympathy of an onlooker in the joyous words, "I roast my chickens to the glory of God." This simple saint knew to the full the stark significance of the dreadful words, "If then the light in you is darkness, how great is that darkness!" Glimpsing tomorrow, one sees a tomb, like that of an Egyptian Pharoah, filled with gold and harps and books and tools (all the paraphernalia of an ambitious life) and in the midst a skeleton—all that the man is; for his chosen gods have taken him to themselves. Man may choose such an earthly heaven if he wills.

Our Lord intensifies the warning. "No one can serve two masters; for either he will hate the one and love the other, or he will be devoted to the one and despise the other. You cannot serve God and mammon" (Matt. 6:24). If the words *love* and *hate* seem too strong, it should be realized that in this usage they are without emotional content. Our Lord is going behind the outward expression of these things and deep into the roots under them. He has in mind the initial decision of the will which ultimately results in love or in hatred. And for us, as for all men, there is but one alternative. We must choose between devotion to God and slavery to "the mammon of unrighteousness." Here *mammon* means money, the love of which is "the root of all evil." Not that money can ever be evil in itself, not that it cannot be put to the noblest of uses, but that its possession is always a secondary matter to the Christian, always no more than the tool of a higher purpose. He does not care much about it. He is dedicated to the service of God. He must carry the torch of man's redemption.

How We Can Avoid Anxiety:
Matthew 6:25-34

The reader will find a comparison of Matthew 6: 25-34 with St. Luke's report of the same sayings (12:22-31) well worth while. Both statements deal with the folly of anxiety, a condition, neither necessary nor useful, which, if psychology has taught us anything, can be emotionally and even mentally disastrous. But the subject is difficult, and counsel about it is quite often ill received. Yet Jesus, as though looking far beyond the range of the disciples under the immediate spell of His person and into the pallid faith of our sceptical era, uses the simple, practical illustrations drawn from "worries" familiar to us.

In meeting the problem of anxiety, Jesus does not at first lift us into a high spiritual realm. In effect He says, "Why worry about your clothes and your food? Isn't your life—your simple physical life—the important thing?" In one picture after another, He demonstrates from nature itself the loving care of the Father for all His creatures and then goes on to say, "If God so clothes the grass of the field . . . will he not much more clothe you, O men of little faith? Therefore do not be anxious, saying, 'What shall we eat?' or 'What shall we drink?' or 'What shall we wear?' For the Gentiles seek all these things; and your heavenly Father knows that you need them all. But seek first his kingdom and his righteousness, and all these things will be yours as well."

Jesus' answer to the problem of anxiety is at once a challenge to our faith in God and the primary security of heart and mind that the Faith affords. The Gentiles, helpless devotees of a confused and hopeless heathenism, succumb to the worldly anxieties which obsess men who have no resort to the Father. But believers know that they can trust Him for the immediate, real necessities. They must not be distracted by the pressures of the moment. They must, if they would have emotional and spiritual security, spend themselves in the fulfillment of His will.

Having finished with illustration, Jesus concludes His teaching about anxiety with the counsel: "Therefore do not be anxious about tomorrow, for tomorrow will be anxious for itself. Let the day's own trouble be sufficient for the day" (Matt. 6:34). This final sentence, the issue of a moving pity for the confused and frightened pagan world of men, stresses at once the foolishness and the wrongness of any preoccupation with the supposed troubles of tomorrow. After all, who can know the course of tomorrow's events? And who may hope to cope with them if he permits a heartbreaking anxiety to wreck the duties of the present hour? The mastery of today's problems is all that is within the capacity of normal men and women.

The mastery of today's problems, each duty well

and completely done, is the one adequate preparation for the unforseeable happenings of a future still secreted in the mind of God. This, of course, is an eminently practical bit of psychology by which even the pure secularist may hold his peace of mind until the tensions grow too strong for the fibres of his heart. But the Christian is not left with the merely human resources that the psychologist may supply him. He does not, if his faith be true, follow the flickering candle of man's genius. In seeking "his kingdom and his righteousness," believing man pursues the Flame which alone can light the roads of life shadowed by the darkness of the sins of men. For this is no prophet who speaks to us, no man wiser than the wisest of us all. This is the Eternal Incarnate Lord, Creator, Redeemer, Master of Life, who holds out to us for the taking the keys of His Kingdom.

Chapter VI

NEW ANSWERS TO OLD QUESTIONS

Matthew 7

Even the most casual reader, moving out of the sixth into the seventh of St. Matthew's chapters, will be halted by the abrupt change of tone and substance. Certainly Chapter Seven is not a continuation of the preceding chapter. Certainly, especially when read aloud, it has the sound of a series of replies to unconnected questions rather than the sound of a continuous discourse. And that, probably, is what it is. Even conservative scholars seldom tempted to speculation are inclined to believe that these "answerings" originally came immediately after Chapter Five. At any rate that chapter and Chapter Seven belong to the earliest of the written sources, and it is highly probable that after the tremendous, revolutionary statements reported in the earlier passage, our Lord was interrupted by a barrage of questions demanding immediate attention. He had paused after His startling injunctions concerning divorce and the love of enemies. Inevitably He would have to meet not only the queries thus provoked, but the objections of disturbed disciples. After all, they were hearing an unprecedented message. After all, it was imperative that these men, the twelve in training, should be thoroughly schooled in the creative principles of The Way.

Jesus' moral requirements and spiritual insights in Chapter Seven move at a level far too high for a mixed crowd of Palestinian Jews. Obviously they were intended as the primary essential discipline for these carefully selected men who were to be the pioneers of the reformed religion. And this reformation was at once one of correction and illumination. The Jews were to be brought to a full realization of the true prophetic significance of their historic Faith. They were, in accepting Him as "the Light of the world," to fulfill their ancient function as "the Chosen People, the People of God." Historically, the rejection of the Messiah by His own people was yet to come. In the minds of the compilers of the Gospels this had long since occurred, and the written record had become the powerful instrument for the conversion of the Gentile world. Now the spiritual and moral disciplines, first designed for the Apostles as they built the walls of the New Israel on the repointed foundations of the Old, have become the very fabric of the young Church's life and the basic principles of our behavior today and forever. This is Church discipline, incapable of correction or modification by the hands of men. It is our rule of life.

The Standard of Judgment:
Matthew 7:1-5. Luke 6:37-42

"Judge not, that you be not judged. For with the judgment you pronounce you will be judged, and the measure you give will be the measure you get" (Matt. 7:1-2).

No doubt some among His hearers had, understandingly enough, been overcritical of others. The saying is based on a familiar old Hebrew proverb which they must have known. Jesus has just said to them, "Blessed are the merciful, for they shall obtain mercy" (Matt. 5:7). Now He reminds them in even stronger terms that they, before the throne of the Eternal Judge if not in the span of their earthly lives, will be judged by the precise standards which they have set up in their judgment of others. This should halt the Christian at that very moment when he begins to think critically of those whose external conduct provokes him when he cannot know their inner motives. Above all, this should block his public condemnation of others in forgetfulness of that quality of mercy and of compassion characteristic of the true disciple; and it should bring him to an exacting self-examination of his own weaknesses. Here, again, is an assault upon the basic sin of pride, that pride which blinds the individual to those sins and weaknesses in himself which in others he so clearly sees, or seems to see. And so—"Why do you see the speck that is in your brother's eye, but do not notice the log that is in your own eye? Or how can you say to your brother, 'Let me take the speck out of your eye,' when there is the log in your own eye? You hypocrite, first take the log out of your own eye, and then you will see clearly to take the speck out of your brother's eye" (Matt. 7:3-5).

This superb bit of dialectic, humorously ironical, strikes to the root of the trouble. One is reminded of that single remark of Jesus, the climax of an overwhelming unspoken drama, "Let him who is without sin cast the first stone." Here, as there, the people are compelled to see in themselves those very sins and weaknesses which they are so swift to condemn in lesser replicas of themselves. This, of course, is a familiar diagnosis in modern psychology which may be said to err chiefly when it departs from the ultimate principles of Jesus in both analysis and method. But here is more than a psychic maladjustment unconsciously acquired. Here is a prideful act of the will that will succumb only to the most rigorous of treatments, and our Lord does not hesitate to expose hypocrisy when its presence is certain. Yet the total picture, a mode of healing linked with diagnosis in subtle and decisive fashion, becomes clear when St. Matthew and St. Luke are read together. In verses 39 and 40 of the latter, the self-righteous judging of others is attributed to a remediable moral and spiritual blindness: "Can a blind man lead a blind man? Will they not

both fall into a pit?" Then, in compassionate consideration of these trembling, frightened disciples caught
in the chilling sense of guilt, the remedy comes in-
stantly: "A disciple is not above his teacher, but every
one when he is fully taught will be like his teacher."
And this is but another way of saying, "I am the Way,
the Truth, and the Life." In the following of *The
Teacher* rests the secret of redemption.

The isolated Matthean saying, "Do not give dogs
what is holy; and do not throw your pearls before
swine, lest they trample them under foot and turn to
attack you" (Matt. 7:6), found nowhere else in the
Gospels, is sober counsel given, no doubt, in response
to the anxious questioning of disciples anticipating
wasted efforts upon unresponsive people.

Although it is true that in old Israel meat offered
in sacrifices was consumed by the priests because it
had been put to a sacred use, we can hardly assume
that Jesus merely intended to remind converts from
Judaism of this familiar prohibition. To be sure, "the
dogs" were scavengers and seldom pets, and pigs were
forbidden as a source of food. Hence Matthew 7:6
can only be a symbolic picturization of the waste and
folly of exposing the precious things of the Gospel
and the Church to those who will scorn and profane
them. Certainly, as these preaching-teachers strike out
in their crusade to win an alien world to the obedience of its Redeemer, they will crash head on with

bitter foes who, with ears deaf to the truth, will attack
and profane them and their message. It is as though
one were to attempt to proclaim the Gospel to a
meeting of atheistic Communists schooled in the
hatred of Christ. But this is not to say that one never
should attempt to win such persons. Evangelism is
ever fraught with danger and with death as the fate
of many a missionary in Korea and in China amply
proves. The disciple is to be courageous to the point
of risk and faithful in the face of the bitterest of
enmities. Never is he to seek martyrdom when nothing is to be gained for Christ and the Kingdom. Never
is he to provoke enmity by worthless stubbornness.
Never is he to parade as a hero for mere heroism's
sake.

An Interlude on Prayer and Love:
Matthew 7:7-12

It is not improbable that, in St. Matthew's source,
this section followed the Lord's Prayer and the subsequent strictures upon man's forgiveness of man as
the price of his pardon. Inevitably doubts and questionings would have developed as they do today. Men,
caught in the desperate tensions of a world not less
hard than our own, would have cried out for further
guidance. To them, as to us, the requirements for a
place in the Kingdom must have seemed well-nigh impossible of achievement. How could ordinary persons,
impelled by the unsought pressures of personal and

social and political conflict, ever hope to climb to this degree of perfection? Believing men always are confronted with this dilemma, whether as individuals or as groups; for the Christian is ever in crisis provoked by the insistent challenge of his faith to all other ways of belief and of life. And in such moments, when mind and spirit threaten to sink into despair, he needs the reminder that when Christianity is in its deepest crises its brightest opportunity is at hand. That is the record of the Church's age-long history, a history which one of the greatest of modern historians has named "the finest cordial for drooping spirits."

The psychology of faith, however, is far more than a group psychology. Man is gregarious in his joys, but desperately solitary in his griefs, especially when these are the consequences of his sins. But our Lord, living that man may never be alone, neither permits him to be tempted beyond his strengths nor grieved beyond relief and remedy: "Does your heart condemn you? God is greater than your heart!" Thus He shoulders, as He did His cross, the burden of that sinfulness and sorrow that we cannot carry alone. He will not tolerate a guilt complex nor allow the final breaking of a heart.

In a sudden deep reading of human need, Jesus brings to us the key to the solution of our problems in illustrative form: "Ask, and it will be given you; seek and you will find; knock, and it will be opened to you. For every one who asks receives, and he who

seeks finds, and to him who knocks it will be opened."
Here is another and confirming revelation of "the
utter accessibility of God." Its one technique is the
crying of the heart to whose every thought and hope
and need the mind of the Eternal Trinity is ever
tuned. And this is brought home in a sequence of the
humblest of pictures drawn from the life of every one
of us: "Or what man of you, if his son asks for a loaf,
will give him a stone? Or if he asks for a fish, will
give him a serpent?"

The kindliness of a good father for the son of his
love is infinitely outstripped by the compassion of our
heavenly Father for His children: "If you, then, who
are evil, know how to give good gifts to your children,
how much more will your Father who is in heaven
give good things to them that ask him?" Then comes
the gentle reminder, a connective with the early words
about judging others: "So whatever you wish that
men would do to you, do so to them; for this is the
law and the prophets." The measure of what we do
for men is the measure of what we may ask of God.
Yet, as Jesus puts it in the Parable of the Sower, His
measure to us will not be conditioned by the miserli-
ness of men. It will be "full, pressed down, and run-
ning over." In a word, the prize for which the believer
seeks—his place in the Kingdom of the redeemed—is
to be won by prayer and effort without ceasing. And
so we grow into, and through, the *agápê* of the Father.

And Now Our Lord Sums Up:
Matthew 7:13-29

Suddenly, after gentle explanatory phrases, Jesus strikes what seems to be a note of hardness. But His strong words in Matthew 7:13 ff. must not be divorced from their context—the full fabric of the whole revelation of the four Gospels plus the lucid interpretations to be found in the letters of St. Paul and in the other Epistles. Yet even sentimental readers cannot escape the sense of urgency which permeates the personal and social disciplines of the Sermon. Christianity is neither a simple nor an easy faith. Its disciples embrace it only after a complete awareness of its difficulties and its hardships. Not for nothing did Jesus say, "Take up thy cross and follow me!" Not for a moment did He imply that this new discipleship was to offer protection from the desperate sacrifices and sufferings that always characterize a pioneering movement. And this pioneering was to endure through the whole process of history, a process in which all things were to be made new. The ideal spread before men in the Sermon on the Mount is to be won only through an unrelenting tenacity of purpose. Compromise is stricken from this luminous portrayal of the Christian ethic—all compromise except the divine compromise of mercy, through which the Christian character reaches toward its noblest peak.

So Jesus, in a striking parallelism, paints the picture: "Enter by the narrow gate; for the gate is wide and the way is easy, that leads to destruction, and those who enter by it are many. For the gate is narrow and the way is hard, that leads to life, and those who find it are few." As these words are being written it is night. The writer has just come from a heart-rending procession of conferences with a group of unrelated people, young and old, who in the mad, stupid rush of a great city's chaotic life saw the tempting ease of the "wide gate" and so plunged into the path of destruction. Whole families, the innocent with the guilty, are involved in the folly of a few youths who never had been shown "the narrow gate" and "the hard road" which leads to life. These will be turned back, no doubt, and so suffering will have served its salutary purpose in a blessed humbling of pride and self-will. But the stark tragedy is that so few of us ever see "the narrow gate" opening upon the path "that leads to life," and so the spirit dies. Yet that "narrow gate" and that "hard path" are brilliantly lighted by the words and example of "the Word made Flesh." We have been freed from uncertainty. The road map of the redeemed life has been spread before our eyes.

Yet nothing could be more clear than the fact that this is not a severe admonition to the following of an ethical code. Jesus has not suddenly fallen into the pharisaic error that He had so vigorously condemned, and of which modern churches have been guilty. No, this is a tremendously reinforced reminder that the whole process of redemption hangs upon the unquestioning acceptance of Christ. It is life under His mastery that is the narrow gate and the hard path, for man's willfulness ever tempts him to compromise when vital moral and spiritual issues are at stake. And, at the same time, this is an inescapable challenge to the Christian to extend himself in the spreading of the Good News to all men everywhere. The imitation of Christ, an impossible behavior without incessant resort to prayer and worship, is the one certain way by which the Gospel may be spread despite the pitfalls that lie before us. And these pitfalls are many and, sometimes, within the very body of the Church herself. Our Lord deals with some of the most deadly.

"Beware of false prophets, who come to you in sheep's clothing but inwardly are ravenous wolves." In an age in which a thousand pseudo-philosophies and false religions contend for the allegiance of all men, this warning assumes a new significance. Certainly, at the moment of His speaking Jesus had in the forefront of His mind those evil persons who, with neither faith nor conscience, turn the religious instincts of men to their own uses. Nothing could be more contemptible. Certainly, too, His warning may be applied to that multitude of well-intentioned teachers and healers who offer their arts for the mending of broken minds and spirits when, in truth, nothing can suffice but an unwavering faith in the Lord of Life. Often these secondaries are valuable aids to the physician of the soul; never are they to be mistaken as the final curative of spiritual and moral ills. But perhaps the false prophets whose activities are most perilous are those within the fabric of the Church whose teaching, deliberately or ignorantly, misapplies the real message of our Lord. Even before the writing of the New Testament was finished, these heretics had begun to create difficulties. St. John's Gospel was in part a contention against the Gnostics who held false views about the nature of the Incarnate Christ, and Gnosticism has appeared in a variety of forms in every generation since. "You will know them by their fruits . . ." is a cue to their recognition, a thought even more beautifully expressed by St. Luke (6:43-45) in a slightly different context.

After the warning about false prophets, Jesus, perhaps acutely conscious of His own experience with timeserving religionists who gave lip-service to the Father while their hearts were elsewhere, launches into a warning that has seldom been more pertinent than at this hour of Christian history when the forms of worship so often are offered for the substance, when money is given as a substitute for self, when the meticulous performance of rituals and ceremonials replaces the adoration of the heart, when the rostrums of human societies are accepted in lieu of the altars of the Body of Christ:

Not every one who says to me, "Lord, Lord," shall enter the kingdom of heaven, but he who does the will of my Father who is in heaven. On that day many will say to me, "Lord, Lord, did we not prophesy in your name, and cast out demons in your name, and do mighty works in your name?" And then will I declare to them, "I never knew you; depart from me, you evildoers."

Always it should be remembered that "the kingdom of heaven" is post-historical in meaning throughout the great Sermon. It has to do with the abode of the faithful after the final coming of the Lord "in power and great glory to judge both the living and the dead." Those who are condemned are they who in pride and self-will have substituted personal religious philosophies of life for the course prescribed by the King Himself. Of course, it is both morally and practically impossible for us to identify these individuals. We have no access to the inner secrets of men's hearts, no knowledge of their strains and stresses, and thus no capacity for that judgment which the Lord reserves for Himself. As we read Jesus' striking words we may well experience a sudden consciousness that they are meant for us. Have we taken pride in our achievements for both man and God? Have we loved the praises of our fellows for "the mighty works" done in the Holy Name? Have we become content with having done that—all of that!—which we believe to have been our duty? Then our state is perilous indeed, because the dominant characteristics of the Christian

life are an utter discontent with accomplishment and
an engulfing sense of sinfulness: *"Oh, that I might
be delivered from the body of this death!"* So our
struggle is for the true humility of holiness, a perfect
oneness with the purposes of Christ.

Then, having "taught them as one who had authority, and not as their scribes," our Lord ends the
Sermon with a movingly dramatic story reported in
both St. Luke and St. Matthew. It is a tale which
treats of the choice that every man must make, the
choice between the joy and the glory of the life of
Faith and the way that leads to death. So vividly, so
completely is it told that further comment and illustration is superfluous:

> Every one then who hears these words of mine and
> does them will be like a wise man who built his house
> upon the rock; and the rain fell, and the floods came, and
> the winds blew and beat upon that house, but it did not
> fall, because it had been founded on the rock. And every
> one who hears these words of mine and does not do them
> will be like a foolish man who built his house upon the
> sand; and the rain fell, and the floods came, and the
> winds blew and beat against that house, and it fell;
> and great was the fall of it.

167-1055-C-5